The Country Doctor's Wife

By Ora Lewis Bradley

Originally published by
House of Field, Inc. New York

Original Copyright MCMXL by Ora Lewis Bradley

Transcribed by D.L. Gilmore

Re-release Copyright 2014 D. L. Gilmore

TRANSCRIBER'S NOTE

ORA LEWIS BRADLEY was my wife's, Susan Louise Hobson Gilmore, great-grandmother. She wrote two books to my knowledge: her autobiography, <u>The Country Doctor's Wife</u>, and a novella, <u>A Rose by Any Other Name</u>, the story of a young lady who marries a man who turns out to be an outlaw.

<u>The Country Doctor's Wife</u> was published by Mrs. Bradley in 1940. There were a limited number of books printed. Over the years, the number of her descendants increased and many have not seen this book; or they have seen it, but do not have a copy of their own. For that purpose, I transcribed and am republishing this book.

Mrs. Bradley's book is a well-told story of life in Northwest Georgia from the Civil War into the 1930's. It gives the reader a window into the world of that time. There is history in this book that you simply will not find in any text book and in very few other histories. Whether it's her descriptions of the hidden ear of red corn or of playing with tumblebugs (dung beetles) or her honest portrayal of the meanness that children can exact each other, Mrs. Bradley wrote well and wrote with humor and self-deprecation and a great eye for the world around her.

The story is also a love story, the love of Mrs. Bradley for her husband of her love for her children and her family. And it is a biography of her husband, Dr. Richard S. Bradley.

Some readers might find some language to be insensitive by 21st Century standards. Do not judge the past or folk from the past by present day mores. It's not fair or intellectually or morally honest. Do not let your own opinions get in the way of Mrs. Bradley's story, because her story is a good and important one that should be known.

The book has been transcribed as it was written. The original font was changed to make it more compatible with the publisher and I have added editor's notes in some places where I thought it would be helpful to the reader. I have rarely changed spelling or grammar and have tried to faithfully copy exactly what Mrs. Bradley put on paper, with some corrections where there were obvious typeset errors in the original. I apologize to the reader for my own errors.

I want to dedicate this re-publication of Mrs. Bradley's wonderful book to three of her grandchildren: Dick Bradley of Fort Worth, Texas (named for his grandfather, the Country Doctor), my mother-in-law, Dot Bradley Hobson, who regrettably is no longer with us, and Anna

Bradley Mcearchern of Mesa, Arizona. I wish I had republished this book before Dot's passing.

I hope you enjoy Mrs. Bradley's story as much as I have.

- Doug Gilmore   September 30, 2014

The Country Doctor's Wife

Dedicated to

MY DEAR CHILDREN

Dicksie
Crisp
Lois
Agnes
Jefferson
Richard
Lurlyne

TABLE OF CONTENTS

I. THE OLD FASHIONED COUNTRY DOCTOR	1
II. BACKGROUND	3
III. CHILDHOOD RECOLLECTIONS	11
IV. VISITING KINSFOLK	39
V. WAR BETWEEN THE STATES	47
VI. SCHOOL DAYS	55
VII. THINGS SOCIAL AND RELIGIOUS	63
VIII. COURTSHIP AND MARRIAGE	77
IX. EARLY MARRIED LIFE	83
X: WAITING FOR THE DOCTOR	89
XI: DREADED DISEASES	97
XII: A FROLIC	107
XIII: CASES	111
XIV: BILLS	131
XV: PRENATAL IMPRESSIONS	135
XVI: ROMANCE AND TRAGEDY	137
XVII: SUPERSTITIONS AND INCIDENTS	147
XVIII: OUR OWN FAMILY	151
XIX: SICKNESS AND SORROW	163
Madrigal	169
XX: MOTHER	171
A Tribute to My Mother	171
Carriages	175

XXI: POLITICS	177
XXII: TRANSPORTATION	181
XXIII: WORLD WAR	185
My Memory Pictures	191
XXIV: GOLDEN WEDDING	195
XXV: EVENING OF LIFE	197
Autumn	197
What I like Best About My Pastor	198
XXVI: LOOKING BACKWARD	201
XXVII: PHILOSOPHY OF LIFE	217

I. THE OLD FASHIONED COUNTRY DOCTOR

COUNTRY LIFE in the South will never again be as it was three and four score years ago, when the doctor and I entered the world.

The country itself has changed. The stately pines that crested the "rosy-cheeked hills" of North Georgia have disappeared. Once fertile fields have washed into gullies, while paved highways have taken the place of the old rough mountain roads.

The old-fashioned country doctor, that faithful servant of the people, riding down the "big road" on horseback, later in high-topped buggy drawn by the four-legged companion of his long, lonely trips about the country neighborhood is fast disappearing.

This familiar figure, who will soon ride only in the land of memory, looked every inch a doctor, and smelled like one, too, with his tinctures, squills, powders and oil of lavender. He had to furnish all his medicines, mix his own powders and roll his own pills, for there were no drug stores within reach. Instead of writing prescriptions, the doctor "dosed out" medicine with his pocket-knife, and folded it into little papers.

While present-day doctors glide along in heated limousines over paved highways, the old country doctor of fifty years ago saddled his tired horse and, facing stinging north winds, rode over frozen or snow-covered roads that in many places were hardly more than rough, winding trails among valleys and hills.

A sketch of Dr. M.J. Dudley, my husband's preceptor, will not be inappropriate here. Dr. Dudley was a real pioneer, known all over this part of the country. He was a low, fat man, with long snow-white hair hanging down onto his shoulders. For years he rode a big white horse named Fed. Sometimes in traveling over lonely country roads at night the doctor would became lost. Then he would give old Fed the rein, and he would carry his master safely home. When this faithful horse became too old to travel he was not turned out to die. Instead, he was fed, pampered and cared for just as when he did regular work, and when he died of old age, was given a decent burial.

Dr. Dudley lived in Sonoraville, and perhaps did the largest practice of anyone in his day. He loved his dram, and sometimes he imbibed too freely. When he did that he was full of joy and fun. I remember when he was elected to the legislature, and on his return he sipped a little too much. When his beautiful wife Julia went out to meet him, he laughed heartily and said, "Now, flower, run back into the house. I'm fine. I'll be right on."

Old Dr. Dudley was considered the best doctor in all the country. When he rode down the road on old Fed, with all his powders and tinctures, ipecac, podophyllin, valerian, oil of peppermint, and vermifuge, you could smell him for quite a distance. Pioneer doctors used strong medicines. He was our family doctor, and was there when I and all the other children were born.

II. BACKGROUND

THE DOCTOR was born October 31st, 1857, in the southern end of Gordon County. I was born October 18th, 1869, in the northern end of Bartow County, Georgia, our homes being just five miles apart. We both came from old Colonial stock, and our ancestors fought in the Revolution.

The doctor was the seventh son of Reverend Burton Bradley, an old-fashioned, hard-as-steel, missionary Baptist preacher, and Theresa Costephens, who migrated to what was then called Cass County[1], Georgia from North Carolina, though the family came originally from Virginia.

His great-grandfather had come to this country from Wales as a stowaway on a ship. Family tradition says that some children were playing on a wharf alongside which lay a vessel making ready to sail. Unnoticed, a little boy about three years old crept into a quiet place on the ship and fell asleep. Sound asleep. The ship was well out to sea when he woke and came out. Too far to put back just to return a baby to his mother.

When he arrived in a Virginia seaport, a kindly family took the child and raised him. From his limited speech, they understood his name to be Bradley. They called him James. James Bradley grew to manhood, fought in the Revolution in

---

[1] *Transcriber's Note: Cass County was later divided into four counties, two of which are the present day Gordon and Bartow.*

Virginia under General George Washington, married, and moved to North Carolina where he became a good citizen.

The doctor's grandfather was an honored citizen of North Carolina, serving as justice of the peace, and a member of the legislature.

Burton Bradley, father of Dick, preached the gospel and organized churches throughout Gordon County for sixty years, making no charge for his services. All he ever received in money was one silver dollar, which a man handed him at the close of a great revival meeting. In those days "salvation was free". One reason was, there was very little money in circulation, in the South.

But he, his wife and family were very industrious on their farm, so in time they prospered. Four sons, John, James, Richard, and Jefferson graduated from Emory College, three becoming doctors. At his death Rev. Bradley left a valuable plantation to his heirs.

The way was very hard; well did the doctor remember the privations of the war between the states. They took old plow points, all the tools they had to work with, fashioned them into rude hoes. Providence smiled on them and gave them good crops. Seven-year-old Dick had to mind the calf, while his mother milked the cow which his father had had such a hard time getting. But with so many children, they had to have milk.

Dick's little bare feet used to get so cold on frosty mornings, but it helped some if he could stand in the warm place where the cow had lain during the night. Winter was more than half gone before he could have his new brogan shoes. As he was the seventh son his shoes were long coming. Likewise his new jeans pants and coat, as his mother had to spin and weave the cloth that made all their clothes. She sat up past midnight sewing, making coats and pants all by hand. As the older boys had to have theirs first, little Dick had to bide his time.

And that was not all, he had to sit up and hold the tallow candle, so his mother could see how to sew. There were four girls, younger than the boys, who had to be clothed also. Their garments were made of cotton and wool, all woven and made by hand. In those days women and girls wore linsey "balmorals", now it's slips.

No people in the world ever worked harder than our Southerners, after the war between the states. They would have suffered for something to eat, if Providence had not been kind and given them a bountiful crop of berries. Not a berry went to waste. Dewberries and blackberries were gathered from fence rows and creek banks, and were a godsend.

After the Negroes were freed, many of the aristocrats were put to it to get help; some of them who had never done any manual labor in their lives now were forced to go to work.

The doctor's mother was a frail, pretty little woman, with beautiful dark hair, so long that when she sat on a chair to comb it, the ends would lay on the floor. Never a strong woman, the blow of the loss of one son in the battle of 2nd Manassas and another in the army, was almost more than she could bear. She was unable to do the work formerly done by their slaves.

The doctor's father had owned slaves but when they were freed, he advised them to get out and work for themselves. They did but returned often to see "Ole Massa, and Missus."

Mr. Bradley hired Molly, a white woman, to do the work; cooking, washing and ironing, and helping the children. Molly was physically strong, and very kind to the children. When they were hurt, or sick, or just fussy, she would take them up on her lap and sing lullabies, or tell stories. She was about twenty-two years old when she came to them, and seemed to be a very happy young woman.

A Mr. Benton lived in a fine old house nearby, on a plantation. He came to see Molly and asked her if she would like to make a change at more money. Molly replied that of course she would like more money, but Mr. and Mrs. Bradley were kind to her and the work was not hard. Mr. Benton left, but several letters passed between him and Molly. Finally, against the warnings of Mrs. Bradley, who instinctively distrusted the man, Molly left to work for the Bentons.

The Bradleys heard from Molly once in a while through the neighbors. She seemed to be getting along well until about three years passed. Then the whole county was shocked by the most gruesome murder in its history. Something was forever stamped on little Dick's memory.

On November the 20th, 1870, in late afternoon when the sun was going down, Molly was at the wood pile in the Benton's yard, splitting kindling. Suddenly she looked up and said to one of the small boys, "Jim, come here and turn the grindstone for me. I want to sharpen this dull axe."

Jim turned the grindstone 'til Molly, after testing the blade by running her finger along it, told him to go and play.

With the axe concealed under her apron, Molly picked up the splinters and went into her room in the house. She laid the kindling on the hearth and hid the axe under her bed. She prepared supper; washed the dishes as usual, then went to her room. Having kindled a fire she sat beside it 'til about ten o'clock.

In their bedroom Benton and his wife were sleeping side by side. Mrs. Benton, awaking with a start, found her husband with his head split open, blood and brains scattered all over the bed, and discovered Molly, with a bloody axe in one hand, and a torch in the other.

The screams of Mrs. Benton and the children roused the neighbors, and soon a searching posse was scouring the fields and woods. At last Molly was found half dead on the bank of a nearby creek.

Her clothes had been torn to shreds by the underbrush through which she had fled; her hands and feet were bleeding. She had waded the creek for some distance and had dropped exhausted on the bank.

Molly was arrested and put in jail, where it was found she was shortly to become a mother. Her story of Benton's refusal to give her money to defray expenses back to Alabama where she could find a home with an aunt was pitiful and caused much indignation against the murdered man, and pity for Molly.

She was tried, found guilty and sentenced for life. After serving three years, she was pardoned and worked again as a housemaid, finally going to Alabama. Her baby was born in jail and died there.

For years the Benton house was said to be haunted. When folks passed by their way, on dark or rainy nights, a headless ghost would come out and follow passersby to the creek, then disappear into the bushes. Many people claimed to have seen this apparition and tried to outrun it, but never could.

When he was fourteen Dick wanted to go to school. There was no school near. But the boy was not deterred. He had to work so very hard that he had become discouraged. Deciding to leave home and make his own way, he ran away. It grieved his father and his mother almost to death. They did not know where he had gone, but kept telling each other, "He'll be back." Dick was gone six months.

He went to Alabama. It was in the spring and a man hired him to work on a farm. Then he worked at odd jobs, anything he could get. After a time he got mighty homesick for his mother, and made up his mind to come home. Like the prodigal son, he lost no time starting.

Of course he had to walk. When darkness overtook him he walked on 'til he was too tired to go a step farther. He stopped for the night in what he thought was a pasture, where he saw some cattle and sheep, and lying down slept soundly. The sun was shining brightly when he woke, and to his amazement he found himself in a cemetery. What he thought were cattle and sheep were tombstones.

After returning home the boy went to school for eight months, then went west again for several years. Coming home again, he read medicine with Dr. Dudley. Two of his brothers were also studying medicine, and as a house full of children was ever noisy, the boys moved into a log cabin on the place – where they could be quiet and devoted themselves to their books as late at night as they chose. He then attended Southern Medical College in Atlanta (now Emory University), graduating with second honors, and started practicing at once. From then on, never could he quit or get away from his profession.

III. CHILDHOOD RECOLLECTIONS

MY GRANDFATHER, Tarleton Lewis, came to Georgia from South Carolina in the eighteen-thirties. My grandfather, James W. Lewis, and my father, Harlston D. Lewis, came with him.

Tarleton Lewis bought almost all the land between Pine Log and Fairmount, and built his house on a bubbling spring. He and his wife Margaret were very stout. (The Lewises were all large men, tall and broad-shouldered). He weighed 260 pounds, and she, 240. They couldn't buy a buggy sufficiently large for them to sit on the same seat. But he had a special one made and they rode side by side.

Great-grandfather Lewis traded in cattle and slaves, often making trips to Savannah. I have letters written by him to relatives telling of these trips, and the purchasing price paid for "likely" negro boys.

My father, Harlston Lewis, was a well-to-do farmer. He raised four or five hundred bushels of wheat every year and had a thresher and threshed wheat all over the country. Every farmer raised wheat in those days, but now cotton is the only crop. He also operated a sawmill and cotton gin.

He usually carried several hundred dollars in his pocket and he held onto to it too. He spent nothing foolishly for he had struggled too hard after Sherman's march through Georgia for another start in life to see it vanish in the wind.

I remember once he dropped a lot of money in the yard and we children were hunting for it. How we did scratch around in the dirt and leaves! All but a dime was recovered. At last I found it, put my foot on it, and kept scratching around, moving only the other foot. I wanted that dime. But Pa was watching us and noticed that I did not lift up my left foot. "Lift up that foot!" he commanded. My, how heavy that foot was! I could hardly make it stir. But I knew I had to, and my father got his dime. Even if I could have kept it, there was no place to spend money. The village store sold only groceries and calico. Yes, there was a little stick candy.

I was the oldest of Father's second crop of children, and had a dear playmate in my half-sister Janie. She was the youngest of the first half. Her mother died when she was born for need of a doctor. A horse had been run to death seeking a doctor, but when he got there the poor woman was dead.

I can't ever forget when my mother's youngest child was born. The messenger tried to find Dr. Dudley, but was delayed. My father was frightened to death, mother was so bad. After walking the floor for an hour, he went out on a hillside and hollered at the top of his voice "Hoo-ee, Hoo-ee!" He could be heard for a mile or more. I've never heard such a distress call in all my life. He said if they were within hearing, and heard those three calls at two o'clock in the morning, they'd know it meant trouble, and hurry on.

Janie lived at Grandpa Lewis', but that was only a short distance from our house. We lived in a large white house that had six rooms, and was surrounded by large chestnut trees.

One day Janie went with Grandpa to the circus in Cartersville. She saw the show girls ride their horses, and decided then and there to be a show girl and ride horses too.

Grandpa owned a fine mare named Kit, and as Kit was expecting another colt at this particular time, she ran in the grass lot near the barn. Janie saw her golden opportunity and seized it with enthusiasm. Every day I would go to Grandpa's to play with Janie, and we would go to the grass lot and ride old Kit. Janie would ride sitting down, then on her knees, then standing up. Sometimes she would allow me to ride behind her. Around and around the grass lot we would gallop old Kit. Poor thing! She puffed and blew and looked as if she were going to give out. But she didn't, luckily for us. If Grandpa had known anything about our practicing to be show girls on old Kit, it would have been just too bad. But he never found out. We did our practicing while he was away somewhere in the fields at work.

Sometime after Kit's colt came, Grandpa hitched her to a plow to turn the garden, and just as he was ready to drive into the garden we had a cute thought. Janie took her bonnet off and I helped her.

Mother was careful of our complexions. She would cut two slits in the top of our bonnets, pull strands of hair through, braid and tie the hair tightly.

Well, Janie put her bonnet on the colt, tying the strings under his throat and tearing holes for his long ears. He looked like a "booger." He walked up beside his mother, but she failed to recognize her own baby. She squealed and bit him. He ran, and suddenly knowing him, Kit started after him. Soon she had broken loose from the plow. The rattle of the chains scared the colt, and he ran faster and faster, with his mother trying to catch him. Finally, after chasing the colt around the lot, we managed to catch him, Grandpa, Grandma, Janie and I, all being out of breath by that time. We took the bonnet off, and both he and old Kit quieted down. The scene that followed can be imagined by all with a knowledge of the home discipline in those days.

Janie had a pet cat named Edith, but I'm going to spell it Edyth, for she was an aristocrat in feline society. Edyth was brindle in color. She had a long, slender body, an unusually long thin tail, and green eyes; and she had a habit of dining every day on Grandma's little chickens. Grandma, not wanting to have Edyth killed, asked Grandpa to take her to Yarbrough's mill and drop her by the roadside. He put Edyth into a sack, and after crossing Pine Log creek, about eight miles away, he left her. Two weeks later Edyth was back home eating chickens. This time he snatched her from the doorstep, where she sat with bloody mouth and paws after a hearty meal and slammed her against a stump.

"There now, I guess you'll stop eating chickens!" he exclaimed, as he looked at the big cat stretched at his feet,

14

dead. But as he passed the stump a little later Edyth was not there. She had fully recovered, and continued to eat chickens. At last, in desperation, Grandpa tied her in a sack, weighted it with big rocks and threw into the creek. She doubtless stayed this time. No wonder folks believe that a cat has nine lives!

I can never forget the cats we had at our house. I loved them passionately. Old Molly kept us supplied, as every five or six months she had a litter of five or seven kittens. She always wanted us to stay with her when they came, and would follow us around, uttering mournful cries. We had to make her a bed in the back room, and there would she would lie, singing. But soon we had too many cats, so Pa would have the hired man carry them off to the woods and kill them, unknown to us children.

One time I saw him with his arms full of kittens, the prettiest I ever saw.

I ran and grabbed his arm, screaming at the top of my voice. Pa said, "Let her have one." I picked out the prettiest but it broke my heart to have the others killed. When the man came back I went over into the woods and there by a big tree lay six little kittens, dead. I wept bitterly as I laid them in a row, and thought how wicked a deed it was. I covered them with leaves and dirt, gave these innocent victims a funeral and decent burial.

Molly lived to be so old she had no teeth, but she was a fine ratter. I have seen her bring rats so big she could not kill them.

In those days children were required to sit still and keep silent when grown people were talking, and to say, "Yes, sir," and, "No, ma'm;" also to wait for their meals when there was company 'til "grown folks" had left the table. What droves of company we had! With our big family, we could not get around the table, so we children had to wait. Out of two big "fryers", there would be nothing left for us but the back, the neck, and the "rumble seat."

Some parents were, beyond doubt, too strict, and in discipline were often cruel; but it all grew out of their deep consciousness of responsibility for their children and a sincere desire to "raise them right." This austerity and discipline extended to the grandparents and few children dared openly to disregard the requirements of grandparents.

One morning after breakfast at Grandpa Lewis', he said "Janie, I am going to feed the stock." (Horses and mules were called stock.) "You take the slop to Sambo."

"Yes, Grandpa," replied Janie. But she wanted first to show me her new dress. We knew that Grandpa never told us a second time to do anything. However, we also knew it generally took him a long time to do the feeding, and we thought we'd have plenty of time to slop the pig and return before he came back from the barn. But on this particular morning Grandpa stepped livelier than usual, and while we were admiring the dress, he came by the pen and saw that Sambo had not been slopped.

He picked up a dry corn stalk as an instrument for enforcing instant obedience.

At sight of that corn stalk I took to my heels and before my turn came, was half way home. Looking back once in my flight, I saw shucks and fodder flying, and heard Janie crying, "Yes, sir, Grandpa. I'm going to slop Sambo."

Grandpa had a fine big bull that was very dangerous. He was kept by himself in a grass lot with a high fence around it. All the other cattle were turned out on the range. Sometimes old Ferdy would tear down the fence and get out. When he would come down the road, bellowing at the top of his voice, stopping every once in a while, hooking the bank, pawing the dirt and throwing it over his back, we would run as fast as our legs could carry us to the house for protection.

Old Ferdy had short sharp horns, was mouse colored, with a black streak running the length of his body and tail, and red eyes. He was the terror of my life. I dreamed of him at night.

My mother was Martha Linn. I spent many of my childhood days in the home of her parents. Grandfather Linn's house had been built in slavery times, and after the prevailing custom of the time, had a kitchen at some distance from the "big house." The kitchen had an enormous fireplace. As far back as I can remember, there was a stove in the kitchen also, something unusual in those days. The fireplace was supplied with ovens and pots as cooking there was the usual thing.

In this kitchen were a loom, spinning wheel, reel and table. All the food was cooked here and carried to the dining room in the "big house." Between them was a walk-way made of two rows of hewn logs, with wide boards nailed on them. When it rained or stormed it was necessary for members of the family passing between the two buildings carrying food, to use an umbrella.

The smokehouse was twice as far from the kitchen as the kitchen was from the house; and meal, flour and meat were kept in it. All water used at the house was carried from the spring nearly a quarter of a mile away. I mention these things to show how strenuous was the job of keeping house and cooking for a family in those days. Certainly the women of today have much to be thankful for. But slaves did the work then.

Grandfather Linn had been a Major in the Confederate army. I remember tearing up the silver tassels, and playing with the brass buttons that had been on his uniform. I have been told that he worked all night with the wounded on the battlefield of Cassville.

High Sheriff of Bartow County for a long time, he lived in Cartersville and kept the jail. I was about five years old when I began staying with my maternal grandparents, but I remember watching Grandpa handcuff the prisoners, and, with a double-barreled shotgun on his shoulder, march them to the courthouse for trial. I carried many a pan of food to the prisoners. One of my uncles was always with me. The food was cornbread, with streaked meat, gravy and vegetables.

This grandfather loved and kept some fine race horses that won a number of medals and silver pitchers. I have in my possession a pitcher won by one of them.

My father was also a lover of fine horses and owned a beautiful racer that won many medals. I have one of these medals now. This magnificent mare always came home from a race with a blue ribbon on her bridle. Her name was "Quartette." Father bought her when she was six months old and gave $300[2] for her. She was light bay, and her coat was curried and brushed 'til it shone like gold. Father kept her about ten years, and she won every race she entered --- except the last.

Grandmother Linn was a sweet, quiet old lady. I can see her yet sitting in the corner smoking her pipe. Then there was Aunt Dee (Cordelia), the spinster daughter, who was the mainstay of the house, and uncles who spoiled me beyond endurance.

Their old house was often full of company, and I can see those old ladies now, sitting in a circle, all dipping snuff, talking and enjoying themselves.

One day I decided I would try a "dip," thinking snuff must taste good since grown people enjoyed it so much. Aunt Dee

---

[2] *$300 in the 1880's would be roughly equivalent to $7,500 in 2014 dollars.*

warned me of the consequences. But I thought I knew what I was doing. So when the snuffbox made another round, I took a good dip. Soon the house began turning around. I fell out of my chair and had to be put to bed, the sickest I have ever been in my life. That was the extent of my experience with tobacco.

Almost every woman dipped snuff, and every man chewed or used tobacco in some form. My father had a tobacco patch for home use. I squirm yet when I think of those big, fat green worms that infested the tobacco plants.

In my raising, I do not remember children using snuff or tobacco. For one thing, it was too expensive. Now, most boys and girls, too – the pity of it – smoke cigarettes.

We had to work, all of us. When we got a chance to play, we certainly did not need a "paid teacher" to show us how. Grandma Linn and Aunt Dee decided to have a quilting. I was to go up the "big road" and invite all the neighbors to the quilting: the Todds, Moores, Linns, Carlisles, and others, who lived about two miles distant. I was to take little Deanie, with whom I played all the time, with me.

Uncle Lawrence said if he was me, he wouldn't walk up the "big road" with a little Negro, so I refused to go. But Grandma knew how to make me. I made Deanie walk behind me all the way.

July-Ann and Emmaline, two neighboring women, came to help do the baking. Salt-rising light-bread, corn pone and pound cake, had to be cooked the day before. July-Ann had "tizic"[3] and rattled so, that I wanted to cough for her. She mixed the cake and called me to lick the cake batter off her fingers. Bah! I hate cake batter to this day.

Grandma had two quilts in the frames and the women finished them before night, but I had to show off. I got under the quilts and pushed my head up, upsetting things and acting ugly, a regular "Pecks Bad Girl."

Always, after staying at Grandma Linn's, where I had my own way and was spoiled by my uncles and Aunt Dee, I had to have a spanking or two to straighten me out, when I returned home.

Very often my mother would send my sister Lalla and me over to Grandma Lewis' on errands. In the summer time the "big road" was full of tumblebugs[4], all rolling their balls in every direction. Two bugs to every ball, Papa Bug, and Mama Bug. Papa Bug sitting up on top of the ball, riding, while Mama Bug backs up and with her hind legs, rolls them to their destination. Oftentimes they fell in to a deep wagon rut, and could not get out, then the first wagon that came along, would crush them. My sister and I, feeling sorry for them, would lift them out of the ruts and put them over in the ditch, where they would be safe. They were very offensive, and the minute we

---

[3] *Tizic, or phthisic, was used to describe any number of "coughing" ailments, including asthma and other ailments.*
[4] *Tumblebugs were dung beetles:, beetles that fed on and lived in manure. Horses and cattle moving on the roads left manure and the beetles lived in the manure piles.*

entered Grandma's house, she'd turn up her nose and say "My, my! You've been handling those nasty stinking bugs again. Come right out here, this minute, and wash your hands." Out on the back porch was a shelf, on the right end of which was the water bucket, with a long-handled gourd. On the other end was a wash pan. Hanging on the post was a gourd, with the handle cut off and a string tied through some holes to hang it up by, filled with strong, and I mean strong, lye soap. Grandma poured our water; she wouldn't let us touch her gourd. Grandma was the best soap maker in the country.

After scrubbing well with that lye soap, our hands stinging with fire, we wended our way back home, with a piece of Grandma's apple tart which she always kept in her cupboard. We thought Grandma was just a little bit too particular.

Alas! The lowly tumblebug has vanished from the "Old South." With the coming of the automobile, and paved roads, they could not survive.

At night, we always sat around the fire with our knitting. Our big family gathered around a huge pine-knot fire. My father read, the boys whittled. Mother and we girls knitted. Ma would task us with our knitting. She would measure of fifteen yards of thread, from the tip of her nose to the end of her fingers, as far as she could reach. Ma had awful long arms. She would say, "When you knit this you may go and play." We whined, "It's all knit, knit, all the time. I'd rather go without stockings than knit day and night." But we got even. Watching our chance, we'd break off a long piece of thread and poke it down a convenient knot hole in the porch floor. Retribution overtook us when Ma had to sweep the yard with a brush broom. (I never saw a machine-made broom 'til I was grown. We always made ours from broom-straw pulled in the fields, and we broke off twigs from black-gum bushes to sweep the yards with.) Well, a swipe under the porch brought our hidden thread to light, right before Ma's eyes. O yes, we had to account for it. Our playtime was cut short, and our task was eighteen yards of thread to knit instead of fifteen.

We had lots of fun calling up doodle bugs[5], under the eaves of the houses and barns. There were little tiny sand burrowed holes. We'd get down on our knees and call in a chanting voice, "Doodle up doodle bug, your pot's a boiling over, doodle up doodle bug, your pot's a boiling over. We'd repeat it over and over. Soon, we'd see the sand begin to stir in the hole and up would come Mr. Doodle Bug, to see about his pot boiling over. We'd take him out and look at him and tell him he was a fine fellow, then put him back in his home, until we wanted to fool him again, about his pot boiling over.

Little children have to be amused. My mother had all kinds of buttons. She'd put them in a box, thread a needle with a long double thread, make a knot it in – and break the point of the needle so the little ones would not prick their finger. Sometimes we would sit on a pallet and string buttons for an hour, or more. She had buttons of all kinds and colors. A

---

[5] *Doodlebugs: roly-poly or pill bug, a woodlouse.*

garment with buttons on was never discarded. That would be downright extravagant. Every button was saved. I amused my own children the same way.

When Ma went calling on the neighbors in the afternoon, she always carried her work with her. She made whole suits of clothing for the men as there was lots of finger work she could do.

I remember that she kept a sad iron in front of the fire almost all of the time. She had a little pressing board that she lay across her lap to press the seams as they were sewed. She had too much cooking and sewing to do to knit, except at night.

The neighbors also brought their sewing to our house. Once, I remember one of them brought her daughter's new dress and said, "Mrs. Lewis, I've brought Suly's dress along, you work such pretty buttonholes I'd love for you to make them in this dress, there are only eighteen of them, most of her dresses have twenty-five." Poor Ma, she hated working buttonholes more than any other kind of sewing, but she made them. The dress was made "gaybrelle fashion," the style of the time.

In those days, we had stock law. Cattle and hogs were turned out to "range." Hogs were called up once a day and fed a little corn to keep them from wandering off and becoming lost. As Grandpa lived about half a mile from us, we could hear him plainly, calling up his hogs. He was an expert hog caller. Everybody marked their hogs by cutting notches in their ears. Grandpa cut one notch in the right ear of his hogs, and my father cut two notches in his hogs' left ear. Every farmer knew his hogs by his mark.

Sometimes cattle would stray so far off into the woods that we would have to go and hunt them up. One evening the cows did not come home. Three men decided to go find them. The women were to wait at Uncle John's until their husbands returned with the cows. The country was not settled as it now is. There were thousands of acres in woodland; the men would probably be gone all night. The men got lost in the vast woodland. They wandered about all night long and all next day. About sundown the anxious women saw their husbands coming and went down the road to meet them. But the men were so addled they did not recognize their wives and did not know they had reached home.

The cows had calmly returned some time during the night.

When winter came Grandpa always sold a wagonload of pork hogs. One November day he had the Negroes on the place kill and dress the hogs. The following day he planned to get up early, load the hogs on the wagon and take them to Cartersville. While he was getting ready to start, Janie took a sharp knife, slipped into the smokehouse and cut off every hog's tail. When Grandpa saw his pork had been disfigured he was so mad he fairly smoked. "What did you do that for?" he yelled. "You've ruined the look of my hogs. I've great mind to skin you alive. Get out of my sight."

"But Grandpa, I love hog tails," she whimpered. She certainly had all she wanted that time.

Later he killed hogs for home use, and always had his smokehouse full of fine meat.

My oldest sister fixed me up a beautiful hat out of and old one of hers; white leghorn with a wide blue ribbon around the crown. I was just as proud of it as if it had come from Paris. While I was out playing one day, Ma put the sidesaddle on old Mary. When I came around the house, there sat Ma with my sister Lalla crouching behind her. Of all things! She had on MY PRETTY HAT! Down the road they trotted toward the village store. I yelled to Lalla to take off my hat. She just grinned and held on to Ma. So I called that I was going, too, running as fast as I could. Ma tapped old Mary with her riding whip. It was useless for me to run farther. I was never madder in my life, and still think it was a mean trick.

My half-sister Agnes used to stand before the mirror and comb her long black hair and ask "Don't you wish you were as pretty as your sis?"

Of course, I said "Yes." She had that rare type of Southern beauty, tall, trim, a perfect figure (today you'd call it streamlined), blue eyes, fair skin. She was very popular. Every Sunday some young man's horse was hitched at our front gate, often more than one, as the boys in those days did not always make "dates" before they came. Just took things for granted.

One Sunday, early in the afternoon, I saw a young man tieing his horse, also I saw Agnes running out behind the smokehouse. Ma met the young man at the door and invited him in, and I followed. He was good-looking and well dressed.

After talking about the weather a while, he asked, "Mrs. Lewis, is Miss Agnes at home? I'd like to see her."

Poor Ma! She hated to tell a story, but could not let Agnes down. You see, Agnes did not like the man and would not even see him.

Said Ma: "Ah – No, she is not home this afternoon."

I spoke up, "Yes, she is, too. She's right yonder behind the smokehouse. She ran when she saw you coming."

Ma looked as though she would faint. You can always count on fools and children telling the truth, when it is most inconvenient. The young man lost no time getting away from there, and never came again.

Agnes gave me a whipping for that. She was big sister, and whipped us when she thought we needed it. I didn't think I should be punished for telling the truth, but she said I had embarrassed my mother, and her, too.

When I was twelve and Janie fourteen, there was an epidemic of measles sweeping over the country. Pa gave us orders to stay close to home. He said we must go anywhere 'til the epidemic had subsided.

Janie said she wanted to have measles and get it over with. She lived at Grandpa's. So she slipped off for a ride on old Kit, and went right into a home where folks were sick with measles. In other words, she went after it and got it.

Janie was the only one in the family who could milk the cows, though Grandpa could feed them. So Grandma asked me to come over and do the milking for Janie while she was sick. Of course I told her I'd be glad to do it. I'd have to milk our cows first, but it was only half a mile to their house and I could get up a little earlier.

Janie was pretty sick and had to have Dr. Dudley with her. For two weeks I went twice a day and milked several cows for her. Grandma said, "I'll reward you for your trouble."

One day, after Janie recovered, she and Grandma came over for a visit. Grandma had a little package in her hand. I knew it was my 'reward" and was thrilled. Handing it to me, she said "You were so good to come over and milk our cows, I am giving you a little present."

I took it, thanked her, and opened it nervously, for I didn't receive many gifts in those days. It was enough calico to make me a new bonnet, a yard and a half, and cost fifteen cents. I was proud of that bonnet when Ma made it for me.

My father was very strict with us. He had seven girls and, believe me, they didn't gallivant all over the country with their beaux. If they went to a dance or to church at night, it was with their brothers. When their sweethearts came to see them, they came about two or three o'clock in the afternoon, and nine o'clock was the dead line. If they didn't go then we'd hear Pa: "It's nine o'clock and bedtime."

None of his seven girls remained single. All were married between sixteen and twenty years of age. All were good looking and popular, though my mother always told me I was the ugliest baby she had. I *grew out of it*, I hope.

We had one little sister who was a real beauty when she was very young. My sister and I got so tired hearing it that we despised the child. She had light wavy hair, fair skin and soft brown eyes. My sister and I coaxed her out from Ma's sight one day and gave her a whipping. After that Frances (that was the beauty's name) would cling to Ma's skirts and look at us as if we were tigers. But that didn't keep us from giving her a tap now and then. No one ever told us we were pretty! As time went on and folks quit bragging of Frances so much, we became as fond of her as of the other sisters and brothers.

Yes, we were a big family. I think big families are happiest. We could play so many games, from mumble-pet to twistification. We kept a pack of hounds, Dash, Sages, Queen, Nancy, Old Gamer, Blue, and others. The boys hunted rabbits and squirrels, and at night 'possums.

We had a discarded stove under a shed where the boys put the 'possum 'til morning, when they would take him out, kill and dress him. One morning we heard a big commotion in the shed, the boys laughing and daring each other to take the 'possum out. I went down to investigate. I found they were afraid to take the big, six-pound Sir 'Possum out of the stove. He looked gentle enough to me, so I taunted "Afraid of him, are you? Stand back, and I'll take him out."

They gladly stood back, and I reached my hand over to take him by the scruff of the neck. He grabbed my thumb and began chewing on it. I pulled him out, grabbed his upper jaw with my left hand, holding his mouth open. He was growling and threatening to bite again.

"Don't stand there laughing!" I yelled at my brother Wallace. "Help me turn this 'possum loose!" Wallace grabbed him by the tail. I let loose, grabbed a strong pole and said "Put this across his neck. I'm going to break his neck if it's the last thing I do." So he held the tail while I, with a foot on each end of the pole over the 'possum's neck, took hold of the tail and jerked. Crack went his neck. Gladly I watched him die. But I had a very sore thumb for some time. The boys teased me for years about getting 'possum bit.

I was like the Negro on the scaffold waiting to be hanged. In his last statement he said "Dis so am a lesson to me."

This illustrated a 'possum hunt:

SAMBO'S SUNDAY NIGHT 'POSSUM HUNT
I went out huntin' las Sunday night,
To ketch dat 'possum, sho,
Dat bin a-totin' off my chicks,
Fo' de las' six months or mo'.

Dat 'possum take right down de creek,
An' light up a blackjack tree,
An' Tige, my dog, take atter him.

> An' I foller behin', you see.
>
> When I come up wid him, you're right,
> It wahn't no place fo' me.
> Dat t'ing's eyes look like two ball of fiah,
> An' his teeth – but I didn't stay to see.
> I take de neares' cut to home,
> He almos' ketched me. Gee!
>
> It wahn't no 'possum, but de debbil,
> Up dat blackjack tree.
> I jump de stomps, I tore my clo'se,
> How fas' I run, God on'ey knows,
> But de debbil up dat blackjack tree,
> Couln' run fas' enough to ketch up wid me.

A Negro woman in Gordon County was convicted of poisoning a family; killing one, and almost killing others. She was sentenced to be hanged in Calhoun, Georgia, about fifteen miles from where we lived. This was when hangings were public.

My brother Wallace, four years older than I, danced around and said, "I sure am going to that hanging," I wanted to go, too, but Pa would not let me. Wallace was about seventeen, and thought it would be a great sight to actually see a murderess hanged. A great crowd was there. Everyone was tense with excitement. The woman made a last long statement, denying to the very end that she had committed the crime.

Wallace was a nervous wreck when he reached home. Every night it seemed to him that the Negro woman was coming after him. He slept in a room quite a distance from Pa and Ma. Late in the night he'd yell, "Open the door, Ma! I'm coming." Here he'd come, running and fast as he could, and jump into bed with Pa and Ma, trembling and shaking. This went on for weeks. Wallace never wanted to go to another hanging.

When I was growing up, my father took our foot measure and had our shoes made by a regular shoemaker who lived in Adairsville. Pa would spread a paper down on the floor, tell us to stand on it, then make a pencil mark at the toe and heel. He'd measure around the widest part of the foot, give the length, and mark "girl," or "boy," as the case might be. There were eight of us children at the particular time I am telling about. The man got the order mixed up and made mine "boy" shoes. I was so mad I could have died, so I pretended the shoes were too little for me and hurt my feet, though I knew Pa would not get me another pair. He asked gruffly, "Where do they hurt?" I screwed my toes around, stepped gingerly from one foot to the other, and answered, "They're too narrow." "I can soon fix that," said Pa, taking out his knife. "I'll split them. Say how far you think they should be split." "Clear to the toe," I replied.

Pa looked at me hard. "You take them shoes and wear them,' he ordered. "They don' hurt you, and if I hear any more out of you, I'll tan your hide." He meant it. I was furious and said to myself, "D---nd if I'll wear them!" It was the only time I ever cursed in my life.

On election days everybody was at the polls; the blustery man who always tried to show off – he would wait until everybody was there, then drive up in his buggy (there were not many buggies in my childhood days) with his fine fat horse dancing and prancing. Then there was the little fat man who reared back, thrust his hands in his pants pockets, walked up to my father and said, "Lewis, I don't owe a dollar in the world." Lewis replied, "Hiram, I'd rather owe a dollar and have a dollar, than not owe a dollar and have nothing." Everybody laughed, and the fat man hushed up.

I recall when Felton and Lester were running for Congress[6]. Grandpa was for Felton, and Pa was for Lester. Of course we children were for Lester too. On election day we went down the big road and sat under a clump of bushes. We could hear the horses' hoofs. Just before they came into sight we yelled, "Hurrah for Lester!" All of a sudden who should burst into sight but Grandpa.

---

[6] *Judge Lester, from Rome, a "traditional Democrat", ran against the incumbent, Dr. William H. Felton, an "independent Democrat."*
Felton won his election against Lester. Years later, Felton's wife, Rebecca, became the first woman to serve in the U.S. Senate, being appointed to the seat of deceased Senator Thomas Watson. She was sworn in on November 21, 1922. The Senate adjourned on November 22 to make way for the new Senate, making her term the shortest (24 hours) in Senate history.

"You nasty little devils," he stormed. "Get back to that house. Don't let me catch you here again!" We got. Our fun was spoiled for the day.

A great big fat man, with a double chin, was always in attendance at elections and public gatherings, and had a fascination for us because he had but few front teeth, and no molars. He chewed his tobacco on these front snags, and spat 'ambeer" all over his chin. I never saw him but that his chin was covered with it.

When my oldest sister was married she had a big wedding. Lots of folks were there; all of his kinfolks, and all of hers. After the ceremony everybody went into the bridal chamber to congratulate the bride. When they had gone, Janie and I walked in to look over the new brother-in-law. "Aren't you going to kiss your new brother!" he asked. "No!" we said together. "We wouldn't kiss YOU." I started to sit down on a chair, but Janie jerked it from under me, and down I went on the floor. I jumped up and struck her, and of course she wouldn't take that. She slapped me back, and we started to fight. My sister left the room. I knew she had gone to tell Pa. So Janie and I lit out, and kept out of sight for the rest of the evening. We even lost most of our share of the big wedding supper.

Oh, those big wedding suppers! Everything to eat that could be thought of. Someone was kept busy churning syllabub[7] all

---

[7] *Syallabub was a dessert made of cream or cream-rich milk with sugar and, often, flavored with wine which helped curdle, or "clot"*

evening. The day after the wedding was infare day, always held at the home of the groom. Another big dinner, and the young couple was ready to settle down and go to work.

The bride always wore a dove-colored dress trimmed in a lighter shade. Always home-made, for there were no "ready-to-wears" in those days.

On one occasion we had a triple wedding at our house, when two of my sisters and a brother got married at the same time. That was the biggest wedding we ever had.

One of the greatest thrills of my life was when Pa brought home the organ. I was about fourteen then, and could play almost any song by ear. I had small opportunity to study music. A young woman came into our community and taught the neighborhood girls for three months. That was all the training I had.

I helped carry the organ into the house and unbox it. How beautiful it was! Just as soon as it was set up I sat down and began playing. Pa and Ma took their seats in the parlor, and all the family gathered round. I played and we sang almost every song in the book.

One song we dearly loved was, "Jesus of Nazareth Passeth By." We really made music.

---

the milk. It is more commonly known today as clotted cream.

Grandma Lewis was a sad-faced woman. I don't ever remember hearing her laugh. Sometimes she would smile a little, but that was all. And no wonder. When her youngest son was about twenty-two years old, he fell in love with a fine girl. They were engaged to be married, but they quarreled. Uncle Jim, heart-broken, decided to go far away. So he packed his trunk, kissed his mother goodbye, and went to California. I remember Grandma getting letters from him. They were such sweet letters, always beginning, "My Darling Mother." It broke Grandma's heart for him to go, but he said he couldn't stay, after what had happened. He was the baby of the family, and was a fine-looking man. He was tall and straight, had coal-black hair and blue eyes. I remember he had a black beard, trimmed Vandyke fashion. Nearly all men wore beards in those days. He sent Grandma several gold nuggets from California. The girl never married. I was told she died of a broken heart. Uncle Jim went from California to Norway. He wrote many things about the long days in the land of the midnight sun. He traveled all over the world; then came back to California, and wrote many interesting letters about his travels.

It seemed to be a family trait to leave home and rove around. My oldest brother Willy, deciding to leave home, went to Missouri, and was gone three weeks. When he came back, Pa was making syrup. Will walked up to him and said, "Pa, I've got back." Pa said, "Will, I didn't know you'd been gone." "By God you'll know it next time I leave," said Will. It wasn't long until Will went away again. He never came back. He drifted from one place to another. Finally he found Uncle Jim and went with him. They were together in California for quite a while. Grandma had letters from Uncle Jim, and we had letters from Will. Then we ceased to hear from either. Grandma was worried to death about her baby boy, and we were worried about Will. Several years later we had a letter from Will. He was in a small Western town, and had changed his name. Uncle Jim was never heard from again. Something awful had happened, but exactly what, we will never know. My sister had a letter from Will just before my father died, and when she read to him, "Tell Pa I have always respected him,' Pa didn't bat an eyelash, nor say a word, but he was moved. Will said we must never ask him what became of Uncle Jim. Will died several years ago.

IV. VISITING KINSFOLK

AMONG THE MANY KINSFOLK who visited us was Aunt Ruthy Duff, a sister of Grandfather Lewis.

In the spring of 1882 we received a letter saying she was coming. We didn't get our mail but twice a month, when Pa could find time to go to Adairsville, the nearest post office, nine miles away. During the winter when the roads were so terrible it required a whole day to go to town and back.

This letter contained the news that Aunt Ruthy would arrive the following Thursday to make a long visit. And when I say long, I mean long. In those days when your distant relatives made you a visit it was for several months. We children were all excited. We could hardly wait for her arrival.

Mother had old Furdy come and scour the floors, wash window, and make everything scrupulously clean. Aunt Ruthy was an old lady, up in the seventies, very proud and aristocratic. Ma had seen her once before when she visited her brother, Grandpa. It was one of the mysteries of our lives that this time she chose us to visit. Our family was large and lively, ten of us, while at Grandpa's there were only three grown people.

Ma cooked a nice supper, and lectured us about behaving ourselves. When the wagon rolled up to the back door, sure enough, there was Aunt Ruthy sitting high on the seat beside Pa, with all the baggage the wagon could hold. A big trunk, a little trunk, satchels and hatboxes, were piled high. She had a bonnet-hat in the style of the day. Covering her face was a black woolen veil. She wore a black cloak, with heavy gray shawl over that. Father and the boys helped her down from the wagon. We all gathered round, kissed her, and welcomed her to our happy home.

Aunt Ruthy was tall, with dark hair on top of her head (by the constant use of Ayres Hair Vigor) though the knot at the back was white. She wore a tight basque of flowered muslin, with high neck ruching and a long black skirt. Sometimes she wore a lace fichu around her shoulders, and always a large gold breastpin. You'd think her feet, encased in high morocco shoes, were pinned to the bottom of her skirt. Nothing was visible except the dainty toe of her shoe. She had two or three sets of false teeth. One plate of gold was so heavy she could not keep it in her mouth. At night she took her teeth out and put them into a glass of water. Then her nose and chin almost met. She wore a nightcap, which made her look ghostly.

Aunt Ruthy, suffering greatly with rheumatism, wore plasters on the affected areas. She had on seven Alcock's Porous Plasters when she came.

She was very proud, a lady born; had fine clothes and lovely jewelry. We tried to find out how old she was, but she said: "Don't you know it is bad manners to ask one's age" When we asked her how old Cousin Josie was, her answer was always, "She's in her twenties; fully grown." (Pa said he knew Cousin Josie, and she was in her forties.) We children sat with open mouths, drinking in the tales she told of refugeeing in time of war, of the awful epidemic of yellow fever, and all about her own family. Her oldest son, a Colonel in the Confederate army, lived in New York in summer and San Francisco in winter. Her second son was the wealthiest man in the County in which he lived.

Aunt Ruthy had broken her arm sometime before she came to make us a visit. Being crippled she required a great deal of waiting on. My sister Lalla was delegated to the task of dressing and undressing her. She had lots of fun playing tricks on her, slipping a bustle, or hoop skirt on her or putting her skirt on wrong side out. Of course Aunt Ruthy would find out and make her change it, but Lalla made a game out of an otherwise irksome task. And no wonder! Aunty Ruthy was weighted down with clothes. She had on the proverbial long drawers that came to her shoe tops, the old-fashioned chemise, a "squeeze tight" corset, a light linsey petticoat and heavier woolen balmoral, three white-bleaching petticoats, the top one trimmed with home-made tatting, an underbody, then basque and skirt. Sometimes she wore six petticoats.

We children got pretty tired of Aunty Ruthy; she interfered with our playing. Every time we got a chance to play she would call us to do something for her. One day I got the old Blue Back Speller down and read these old wise sayings to her:

"Brass is made of zinc and copper."

"We should not prevaricate nor equivocate, but tell the plain truth."

"Never shut the door with a bang."

"VISITORS SHOULD NOT MAKE THEIR VISITS TOO LONG."

My trick did not work, for she stayed with us almost a year.

During her visit Grandma and Aunt Ruthy planned a trip to Seneca, South Carolina, to visit Grandma's sister, Aunt Naomi Clayton. Aunt Naomi had visited the year before and had brought a beautiful silk dress. I remember the dress was black and white checked. She had raised the worms, spun and woven the cloth, and made the dress all by hand. She won the prize.

The two old ladies were very enthusiastic and happy over their long trip. Lalla fixed Aunt Ruthy up in her best bib and tucker, and Janie had Grandma looking her best.

Janie and I were to stay with Grandpa while they were away. It was the fall of the year and the weather was fine. One day Grandpa walked in and said, "Girls, the cover on my house is getting rotten, I don't think it will last through the winter, so I've decided to have a housecovering. I'm sure I can get enough men to cover it in one day. I think I'll just go ahead and do it while the weather is fine."

"But Grandpa, who'll cook the dinner?" Janie cried in desperation. "It'll take loads of food. Grandma won't be back for two weeks yet."

"There's nothing wrong with you two girls doing it. I'll kill a shoat, and we've got a yard full of big shanghais, plenty of cabbages, potatoes, turnips, apples, and you both can cook pretty good."

So the men were invited to come the following Thursday. Janie and I could not sleep, planning the dinner. We put two tables end to end, and served as fine a dinner as I ever saw. We cooked everything we could think of, and felt so relieved when it was all over. But Grandpa walked in about four o'clock and said "I want you to cook supper for these men."

We nearly fainted. We never dreamed they'd stay to supper. But there was no help for it. We told August and Mack, the two colored men, to catch some more fryers, and we went to work preparing another meal. Janie was fifteen then, and I thirteen. However, Grandpa and the men praised us and said they had never eaten better meals.

After supper Grandpa brought out his cut-glass decanter of fine peach brandy and every man took a "swig" before going home. Then Grandpa went to the barn to attend to the stock.

Janie picked up the decanter and poured herself out about half a glassful, and the same for me. We added some sugar and water and put in a sprig of mint. We drank it all, and then maybe we didn't have fun. We chased each other around the table 'til the table seemed to be chasing us; through the house we ran, and back to the dining room. We felt as light as feathers, and never so happy in our lives, ending with a biscuit battle. We threw them at each other, 'til Janie hit Grandpa on the nose, just as he stepped through the door.

"Hey! Hey!" he snorted. "Get busy and clean up this room and kitchen, and wash the dishes." He was an old man and had had a strenuous day. We, too, had had a hard day and big responsibility and were glad it was over.

Grandma and Aunt Ruthy came back at the scheduled time, reporting a wonderful visit. Grandma was so glad the house-covering was over, and that we girls had acquitted ourselves so well. She never did know how well, and this is the first time it has ever been told.

Very soon after their trip Aunt Ruthy became very sick with "la grippe." Dr. Dudley said she would get well if pneumonia did not develop, but she had a wire sent for her son.

We were thrilled at the prospect of seeing our cousin Will Duff whom she had told us so much about. He was the finest-looking man I had ever seen. Tall and straight, weighing about two hundred pounds, with black hair and blue eyes, and dressed to kill. We had never seen such a dressed up man.

He and Pa had a good time talking over old times, and their war experiences. He had been a Colonel, and my father a 1st Lieutenant in the Confederate Army. Each had been wounded. They were together in the siege of Vicksburg, where they ate mule flesh and were glad to get it.

Aunt Ruthy got well and remained with us for several months longer. All that winter the poor lady was very feeble and was afraid to get out of the house. She suffered from rheumatism, and had Lalla rub her all over with Mustang and

Barker's Liniments, until she smelled like an old-fashioned apothecary shop.

After spending about a year with us, she decided to go back to her daughter in Mississippi. We had become very fond of her, and really hated to see her go.

As I sit in the failing twilight, my thoughts often go back to those golden days of childhood, and to the beloved sister who was my dearest friend and constant playmate. She was a beautiful girl, and married at sixteen. I can see her mounted on a spirited horse, galloping over the Sweet Fields of Eden, her long raven hair floating behind her, her face wreathed in smiles.

Who knows there are not horses in heaven? Who knows that continued life is not granted to those creatures on a lower plane of earthly existence? Elijah went to heaven in a chariot drawn by horse, and John the Divine saw many horses when "the door was opened" and he was permitted to look into heaven.

Janie was the first one to pass beyond the vale – in our big family.

V. WAR BETWEEN THE STATES

IN MY EARLY DAYS everything was dated either before the war, or after the war, meaning the war between the states.

I would listen wide-eyed to stories of the war, but since then I have learned by experience what it means to have sons far away and exposed to the hardships and dangers of war. One of my sons died in the service during the World War.[8]

My people were in the midst of the fighting, during Sherman's march on Atlanta. My grandfather Linn was a Major, and my father a 1st Lieutenant in the Confederate Army.

The doctor's father, a Baptist preacher, was arrested in old Cedar Creek Church, where he and a few women were holding a prayer meeting. He was taken away a prisoner, but was turned loose after a time.

General Joseph E. Johnston, Commander of the Confederate forces in this section, resigned a commission as Brigadier General in the U.S. Army to become a Major General in the Confederate Army. He took charge of the forces at Dalton in the fall of 1863, and went into winter quarters there until May, 1864. He became famous for his retreat before Sherman, from Dalton to Atlanta, where General Hood took charge.

---

[8] *World War I*

While the General was encamped at Dalton sixteen of his men, whose homes were near there, went without permission to see their families. Some beardless youths to see their parents; some young men to see their wives and children. They returned to camp voluntarily, only to be court-martialed as deserters. They were lined up in front of a long trench and faced the firing squad, with the whole army of sixty thousand on the hillside below to witness the execution. These young men did not consider that they had done wrong. They were fighting for home and loved ones. I have stood by that long grave into which these sixteen HEROES, NOT DESERTERS, fell when they were shot. I say it was cold-blooded murder, and would willingly contribute to a fund to mark their grave. To this day nothing except a few sassafras bushes will grow on that spot, where innocent blood was poured out.

Another sad thing happened during this winter. During a revival meeting in the camp a great storm came up and felled a big tree killing twelve men.

The retreat began, and devastation all along the line, of which the following is a typical instance:

A family named Jones lived near Resaca, Georgia, at the time the Yankees advanced on that little town. At home were Mrs. Jones, her daughters, and an old Negro woman; Mr. Jones being in the army.

The women were warned to get out of the way. Frightened out of their wits, they took refuge in a cellar under the house. One daughter declared she would not give up the house to the

Yankees, but when a minie ball clipped off a piece of her ear, she lost no time getting into the cellar.

The Yankees carried off everything they could, and destroyed what they could not take. After the battle of Resaca, tables were used for operating purposes, the officers being operated on in the house, and the soldiers out in the open. Amputated legs and arms were gathered up and buried in shallow trenches. Some places hands and feet stuck out of the dirt. After dark, Mrs. Jones and the Negro women worked until midnight to cover the exposed members with dirt.

Mrs. Jones had a crop of wheat almost ready to gather, but the Yankees burned the rail fence around the field and turned their horses in to feed. After the army had moved on toward Atlanta, Mrs. Jones and the Negro woman took table knives and cut what wheat was left. They beat out the grains with sticks, and put the wheat into tubs of water to float out the chaff. After the grain was dry, they carried it to the mill and had it ground into flour. These women had done their own plowing to make food for themselves. It was hard work for women, but they managed it. One of the girls held the plow, and Aunt Mandy, the Negro, led the horse.

The doctor remembered Sherman's march. He distinctly heard the roar of heavy cannon during the battle of Resaca, May 18th, 1864. The fear and terror of his people could not be forgotten. The great army seemed to cover the earth. They burned house, schools, churches and took everything before them – cattle, hogs, chickens, and all the stock, leaving nothing to make crops with.

When passing the Bradley home soldiers swarmed all over the place. They did not leave so much as a chicken. His mother was left in the home with the little children. They, with two other women, took refuge some distance away, but some officer sent word they wanted dinner cooked. She dared not refuse, so she and the women returned and told them they had no food. The officers provided the food and left some for the family.

The Bradley family did not have a bit of meat for a year.

Reverend and Mrs. Bradley had two sons in the Confederate Army, John and William. One was killed in action. The following letter was received from William:

April 27, 1863

Dear Father:

I will now write you a few lines to let you know that I am well and truly hope these lines may find you and all well.

I received your kind letter on the 25th, which I read with pleasure, and was glad to hear you were all well, but sorry to hear were not stout. I hope you will be blessed with good health again.

I wrote you while we were in Fredricksburg my condition, but I stayed at a private house, and took care of myself, and am most well. I think it was a cold settled on my lungs. I don't know whether I will be able to stand the service or not, but I am determined to go as long as I can. I could get a discharge if I would try. My officers are good to me. When I am not able for duty, they do not impose on me.

I have heard that the news in Georgia was that Crawford was not good to his men, and you will see in the Georgia papers what the Company says about it; as there has been a report from here with the majority of the Company to be put in Georgia.

I have thought since we have been here that we would have no fighting, but I think we will have it to do, for last Friday night about seven hundred yards of our battery where the guards thought the Yankees were throwing up a long breast work during the night, and last night I reckon they started again, for there was heavy firing.

One of the men in our regiment was looking over his bunk; he was behind it. The rest told him he had better not hold his head above the bunk; then he swore he was not afraid. Then one of the Yankees let slip at him and plugged through the head.

There is firing of course continually. Sometimes the Yanks bring boats on the bay, and our men take a crack at them. I have been at our own battery and saw them throw shells at the Yanks' pickets, and when the shells fell, you never saw cats run faster than they did. I thought it was funny, but I don't reckon they thought so. The Yanks are most too hard for our boys on picket, but they won't come out and face the music. When they do come out, though, our men give them the best of the game. I cannot write what I want to, but if I could see you, I could tell you all about it.

Mr. Collins is over today to see us. He is well.

I went over to the 23d, and saw the boys from our settlement. They were all well and looked well. Marian Bell looks like a new man. I wish you could see our breastworks. If anyone that never saw the like of them was out among them, it would almost frighten him.

I have nothing more of importance to write at present.

I will write you again soon. I understand the Yanks are in possession of Fredricksburg since we left there.

Tell all the neighbors the boys are well and hearty.

So no more at present. Farewell.

William C. Bradley,

To Father,

Address care of Colonel Wafford,

Yorkstown, Va.

Co. K.

P.S. The next letter you write put the letter K on it, as there has been some difficulty about getting them unless the letter K, my company, is on it.

W.C.B.

At this time Confederate money was so nearly worthless that it took ten dollars to buy a yard of calico. Soon it was not worthy anything.

Just after the war, when the South was struggling with the terrible conditions of reconstruction days, the aristocrats of this devastated land were put to such a test as seldom comes to a people. Those who lived in Sherman's path as he marched through Georgia were faced with conditions that tested strength of body, mind and soul. Women tenderly reared were forced to hard physical labor, and families that had lived in princely styled were reduced to stark poverty.

VI. SCHOOL DAYS

WHEN I SEE the handsome streamlined schools my grandchildren attend, I think it well for them to hear a little about the old-fashioned country schools.

The country schools were pioneer institutions, but many prominent men were turned out by them. Such men as "Old Hickory" Jackson, Andrew Johnson, Patrick Henry, and thousands of others. Many business men, lawyers, doctors, preachers, statesmen, and politicians never saw the inside of a college, never had any other chance for an education than a country school. Some had little of that.

The old country school, and the old time church do not fit into the fast and glorious day in which we live.

In the old days no one could call out "school butter" without being licked or ducked in the creek, if one were within a mile of the schoolhouse. I don't know what it meant, but schoolboys just would not take it. If there was a fight in school, all concerned got a whipping, whether they were to blame or not.

When I was seven years old I started to school. Every morning except Saturday and Sunday my brother Wallace, Janie and I used to walk two miles and a half to the schoolhouse. Like other children, we trudged through mud and snow, braved rain, wind and cold, sun and heat, and were utterly unconscious of undergoing hardship. I never rode to school. Nobody did. In the first place, it was only two and a half miles, and the stock had to work. When not working they had to rest. People thought nothing of walking eight miles to town with a dozen eggs or a few fryers for sale. Now, children can't walk four blocks to school without complaining. Such things as consolidated school, paved roads, and school busses had never been thought of.

Ma fixed our lunches, and I'll never forget how good they tasted. We had fried pies, "stickies," good country ham and biscuits.

I had to milk two or three cows before starting to school. That meant getting up before daybreak in winter. Sometimes, if slow, I left without my breakfast. I remember one morning the cow kicked the bucket of milk so hard it went up in the air and came down on my head, spilling milk all over me. I was so mad I grabbed up a wagon standard lying nearby on the grown and threw it at the cow with all my might. It didn't touch her, but hit a pig and killed it. I was afraid to tell Pa I had killed his pig, so said the cow had trampled it. He never found out differently.

Our schoolhouse was built on a hill close to old Cedar Creek Church. All the classes were held in one big room, and there were two teachers; one for the primary grades, and one for the higher classes. There were about a hundred pupils in the school. The teachers certainly did not believe in 'sparing the rod and spoiling the child."

In the those days school-teachers seldom had more than a grammar school education themselves; but what they lacked in learning they made up for in zeal. They believed in flogging the children as often as opportunity presented itself, and they were always right. Nearly all children were warned by their parents that a flogging at school would be followed by a flogging at home. Nobody thought of investigating anything the teacher did. This being the case, I said nothing about the two floggings I got at school, as of course, I did not want to get two more at home.

The first thing we had to learn was our A-B-C's. Following that came the a-b-ab's. We even used to sing them, not going up and down in the regular manner, but across the lines to make various syllables. Here is part of the song we made of them:

B-a --- ba.
B-e --- be.
B-i --- bickaby.
B-o --- bo, bickabybo.
B-u --- bu, bickabybobu.
And so on down the line.

The old Smith's Grammar was the first used in this school. It was divided into four parts, orthography, etymology, syntax, and prosody. We had to parse every word according to certain rules, and we had to KNOW the rules.

We used the Blue Back Speller, and Dictionary. Friday afternoons we had spelling bees and speaking. We had to spell the words and give the definition. One day a great big, long-legged gangling boy was given the word ACEPHALOUS (without a head). He got it divided wrongly, and what he said was "a-ceph," a louse with a head. The whole school stood around the wall for the spelling bees. Each pupil was eliminated when he or she missed. One afternoon everybody had been eliminated except another girl and myself. She was given the word "pomegranate," but left out the first "e." I spelled it right and won the bee. Not long after I won again, but everybody declared it was an accident.

One Friday afternoon when we were having speaking a little ornery boy got up and gave a speech which I have never forgotten.

> Said the big black rooster to the little red hen,
> "You haven't laid an egg since God knows when."
> Said the little red hen to the big black rooster,
> "You don't come around as often as you uster."

One afternoon during a short summer session Janie and I were coming from school when the blackest cloud came up. It rained in torrents. The lightning seemed to strike all around us, but we escaped it. There wasn't a dry thread on us when we came to the creek. We waded up and down in the water, and finally sat down in the middle of the creek. Later we looked like a couple of scarecrows with all the muddy water dripping off us as we went along toward home.

One day I brought a great long quill melon[9] to school for my lunch. All morning I sat at my desk thinking how good it

58

would taste. But at noon my melon was gone. Some older girls had taken it to the woods and eaten it. I never saw even the rinds.

I recall that on one occasion the trustees had a great deal of trouble about keeping a teacher. There were some bad boys in school who made it so difficult. One boy about fifteen years of age, an only child raised to have his way and do as he pleased, was the bully of the school.

When Miss Cain was graduated from college and applied for the school the trustees were afraid she could not control it. They thought perhaps a man could do I better than a woman. There were some uncontrollable children who gave lots of trouble.

Miss Cain insisted that they at least give her a trial. Everything went well for two or three days. Then Tobe, the

---

[9] *A quill melon was a yellow-fleshed musk melon, similar to a cantaloupe, but was not round as a cantaloupe is; rather it was long and gourd-like. Quill melons were popular until the 1930s when they fell out of favor.*

A letter from a William N. White of Athens, Georgia to Andrew Jackson Downing (Downing is considered to be the father of American landscaping), dated April 15, 1852 included this description "I enclose you a few seeds of the "Quill Melon," which we think superior to the Rock [cantaloupe], and the best yellow fleshed melon we have tried. If in your climate, it should prove as good, I think you will be pleased with it. It is nearly as good as the green fleshed melon; of a very singular shape, quite large, and exceedingly productive."

bully, could contain himself no longer. He knocked a little fellow down and made his nose bleed. Miss Cain reprimanded Tobe but said she wouldn't punish him that time. The next day he deliberately slapped another boy down, and laughed about it. Miss Cain told Tom Smith to go out and get her a hickory. Having received it, she began talking to Tobe, who laughed and snatched the switch from her hand, saying with an oath, "No! No! You don't whip me, I take no whipping from nobody, 'specially a d— d woman. I'm going home." He jumped out the door and ran home, only a short distance.

Miss Cain said to the pupils, "Boys and girls, be quiet and study your lessons. Tom, go get me another switch. I'll be back in a short while." Tobe was surprised when he saw Miss Cain entering his home. He was telling his mother what a joke he had played on his teacher. His mother enjoyed the tale as much as he.

Miss Cain said, "Tobe, come on. You're coming back to school."

"I've quit school. I'm not going back. Ma, Ma! Don't let her git me."

"Let Tobe alone," ordered his mother. "I'll get his Paw after you. I ain't lettin' him go no more."

But Miss Cain had Tobe by both arms and was pushing him along. She did not let up 'til he was back in school, he bellowing all the time and trying to bite her. She called for her hickory, and still grasping him by one arm, laid it on his back 'til he was exhausted. It was the first time in his life he felt the sting of punishment. He had been too precious to whip.

When Miss Cain finished, she sat him down on the bench, seated herself beside him, and gave him a good lecture. "Why do you act this way, Tobe?" she asked. "You could be such a nice boy, but instead you prefer to be the worst boy in school. If you don't mend your ways you are headed for the chain gang, and lots of trouble. I've punished you. I had to keep my word."

Tobe hung his head and said, "Miss Cain, I don't want to go home. I want to come to school. If you'll let me come back I'll do everything you want me to."

"You don't know if you mean that or not," Miss Cain told him. "One thing is certain. Unless you change your ways, you can't come back. But if you behave yourself and study, you may come. I'll help you all I can."

Tobe never missed a day. He studied hard and was a model pupil. He craved an education and obtained it, made an honorable citizen, and represented his people in the legislature. He always said Miss Cain made a man of him.

We were too close to the war between the states to have an abundance of shoes and clothes. Boys and girls who were almost grown had to go to school barefooted.

The games we played at school! There were Cat, Bull-pen, Molly Bright, Guinea-squat, Ring-around-rosy --- and many others.

One day the teacher, a man, tried to whip a grown boy, who fought back. My brother and I were so scared we ran home. Afterward the boy came to school armed, it was reported, but nothing further came of the matter.

VII. THINGS SOCIAL AND RELIGIOUS

BACK IN THOSE HARD, LEAN YEARS following the Civil War, the people worked hard, knew how to do without, and put their faith in the goodness of God. There was much of innocent pleasure in their lives. The little towns and country neighborhoods had their simple social affairs, when neighbors would gather and, in forgetfulness of life's stern battles, swap stories, talk over the past, dance, and eat sweet potatoes, peanuts, and popcorn.

The men would give log-rollings, house-raisings, house-coverings, wood-choppings, and the women would give quiltings.

The young people had their dances. I remember the boys getting their partners, the fiddlers tuning their instruments, the caller taking his place. With the starting of the music, the dance would begin. The noise of brogan-shod feet on the rough floor could be heard all over the neighborhood, as could the voice of the caller singing, "eight hands up and circle to the left. Honor your partner. All run-away." That old-time fiddle music put juba in your heels and you just had to dance.

Corn-shuckings came in early winter, when the corn had been hauled to the barn ready to be striped of shucks and thrown into the crib. The men and boys would sit around a heap, and the shucking would continue until about ten o'clock, when supper was announced. A jug of whiskey would be hidden in the corn pile, and the man who found the jug got the first drink. At some of the "husking" when a red ear of corn was found, the jug was passed around. That was not often, as there were very few red ears in a big pile of corn.

The Negroes would have their end of the corn heap and their own hidden jug. Of course they watched for the red ear.

When I was growing up, I well remember the corn-shuckings they used to have on my father's and grandfather's plantations. All the men in the community were asked to come on a certain night. The Negroes only wanted to know where the shucking was to be. It was understood they were welcome to come and shuck corn. I loved to hear them singing as they came from different directions, such songs as "ole Dan Tucker."

> Jaybird settin' on a hick'ry lim'-
> He winked at me an' I winked at him.

> Sail away to hebin like a feather in de win',
> A feather in de win', Lawd, a feather in de win'.

> Dance all night wid de bottle in yo' han',
> Jist befo' day gib de fiddler a dram.

While I was writing this I asked the doctor if he remembered how the Negroes used to sing at the old-time corn-shuckings. He said, "Oh, yes, I surely do." Then he told me

Comin' fo' to carry me home.

There were many others too numerous to mention. There's one, however, that they sang that I've never heard since, nor seen in print. It was something like this:

> I'll plow no mo' co'n.
> I'll hoe no mo' cotton.
> I'll dig no mo' pertaters.
> An' when old Lincoln's sojers cum,
> I'll be my own fer niggers.
> *Chorus.*
> O ring o rally, rally,
> ring-o-rally row,
> O ring or rally, dimocrats,
> rally, rin-o-rally row.
> I'll take my golden headed cane,
> an' walk whar I's a mind to,
> An' no policeman foller me, say'n
> "Nigger, whars yo' gwine to?"
> *Chorus.*
> I'll take my fine seegars
> an' smoke dem by de million,
> Go dancin' down to de fancy ball,

What niggers call cotillion.
Chorus.

They made wonderful music. We hear nothing like it these days. Those old darkies have all passed away, but I believe they make heaven happier with their sweet melodies.

When the corn was all shucked, the guest hoisted the host on their shoulders and carried him to the house. Then came the most important part, the big supper. The table fairly groaned under the weight of food. While the men ate, the Negroes carried the shucks to the shuckhouse in large hampers.

The Negro women, Flurdy, Cindy, and Rhoda came along to help with the supper and wash the dishes. At their own table the Negro men would eat their fill of the same kind of food that loaded the white table. On their way homeward, they could be heard singing those melodies that only the Southern Negro knows how to sing.

The doctor often attended these social affairs, for he loved people, and enjoyed simple pleasures.

At the quiltings the women had a good time together. They talked all at once as they stitched.

It has been said, "If you tell a man anything, it goes in one ear and out the other; but if you tell a woman anything, it goes in both ears and out of her mouth."

For all the talking, they would finish two quilts and bind the edges before they went home to feed the chickens, get up the eggs, milk the cows, and get supper.

I remember at one quilting, we had for dinner --- turnip greens and hog jowls cooked together, baked hen and dressing, a boiled ham, stacks of potato custard, apple pie, and a big yellow cake. Coffee was still scarce and high, so we drank spicewood and sassafras tea, both of which were delicious.

Good old summer time was watermelon time, horse apple pie time, fried chicken time, protracted meeting time. Ah, those halcyon days! After crops were laid by, the people were free to give their time and energy to other things than making a living. This time was looked forward to and prepared for, and was a season rich in renewed strength for the stern duties of life.

During July and August the protracted meetings were held. At these, services would be held twice a day; at eleven o'clock in the daytime, and in the early evening. Always the preacher would announce the evening service as beginning at early candlelight. Long before that time the church would be packed with men, women and children. There would be several preachers. First one, and then another would preach.

The people would sing the old songs of the time with a fire and fervor that has no place in present day religious services. The sermons were long and loud, the prayers many and fervent. Mourners would be called to the altar for prayer. Christians would stand thick at the altar, singing, and talking to the mourners. Often there would be much noise and confusion, with women shouting, babies crying, men shaking hands with one another and giving expression to their emotions with loud "amens" or in deep laughter.

A different way prevails at the present time. Often I wonder if it is better than the way of those old Christians who demanded heart-felt religion. Now, people are asked to join the church, and many walk up and unite with even a change of expression on their faces. I wonder if the old times were not better.

In those days people believed in straight Bible preaching that warned of coming death and judgment and called upon the congregation to repent of their sins and get right with God and their fellow men. They sang the old Gospel hymns, everybody joining in. The old mothers in Israel shouted. The fathers shook hands and embraced one another. Sinners on their knees at the altar prayed for mercy. Of late years emotionalism has been criticized. But since emotions are a big and deep part of the human make-up, I, for one, believe in a religion that takes hold on the emotions.

In those days there was singing and praying, and fervent testifying. Every church had its mourner's bench where sinners knelt for prayer, and where they confessed religion. Every church had its Amen Corner where elderly men sat. Many a deep-voiced "Amen" came for that corner while the preacher was preaching. If none of the brethren said "Amen," the preacher was sure to pause in his sermon, turn about in the pulpit, and say, "Brethren, say 'Amen' if you believe I am preaching Bible truth."

The elderly women sat in the opposite corner.

There were other gatherings, such as Sunday school picnics, all-day singings and church meetings, and the Association. At these there would be singing, preaching, talking, and eating. People would come for miles, in two-horse wagons or on horseback. Some walked. Dinner would be spread under the trees and everybody present would be invited to eat.

Country churches had preaching services one Sunday a month. This was called "Meeting Day." On meeting day a long line of vehicles would rattle over the road leading to the church. I have seen people walking bare-footed, carrying their shoes which they would put on just before reaching the building.

The old-fashioned country preacher was paid for his services, like the old-fashioned country doctor, with anything the people had to spare – corn, fodder, hay, potatoes, meat, firewood, and pine knots. I know one preacher who was given a wagonload of gourds, and as he went home, the rattling of the gourds scared his horse so it ran away, scattering the gourds for two miles along the road.

Experience meetings were very common. I've heard some of the finest talks in these meetings. They were inspiring and uplifting. Then, too, I've heard some that were amusing. An old baldheaded man arose and said, "Brethern and Sisters, I want to tell you there's not a hair between me and heaven this morning." And there wasn't.

Another middle-aged man raised up and said, "I believe that every Christian has a definite work to do. You know the Bible says that a tree is known by its fruits. We must do something. We must bear fruit. I've been noticing a fine big tree on the side of the road ever since I was little boy. Its branches spread out in every direction. It is a fine tree, but you know it has never borne any fruit. It's a 'he' mulberry tree. Fine to look at, but no fruit." A ripple of suppressed laughter spread over the church.

During country revivals I have seen men and women rise up with radiant faces, shouting praise to God for salvation. Nobody could doubt the genuineness of their conversion. All their after-life proved its truth.

There was an old preacher in our parts who visited us often. He was long and lank, with a scattered beard and very homely. He drove a tiny mule, so thin you could count every rib. The doctor did this preacher's practice and never charged him anything. One day he and the doctor walked up to the village store. The merchant's little boy asked his mother, "Who is that old 'booger man'?" His mother said, "Hush. You must not say such things. That's a *good man*." Not long after the preacher was again at that store. The little boy looked him over, walked around him, stared in his face. Finally he asked, "Do you live up in heaven?" "No, Bud. Why?" answered the preacher. "Mamma said you is the Good Man."

We never missed going to camp-meeting at Pine Log. I remember when the big tabernacle was built in place of the bush arbor, in 1880. In 1889 the tabernacle was dedicated. Warren A. Candler (afterward Bishop Candler), thirty-two years old at the time, preached the dedication sermon.

During the 1890's this camp-meeting was the most widely attended event in Bartow County. Every livery stable in the town was emptied on the third Sunday in August. The meeting usually started the Thursday before. Buggies, wagons, phaetons, horsebackers, and pedestrians crowded every road leading to Pine Log.

The gay nineties bloomed out in all their glory. At the noon hour tablecloths were spread all over the hillside, and every tent was full. There was plenty of the best food that skilful hands could provide. Happy greeting and handshakings were exchanged among old friends.

On the third Sunday in August, 1895, Dr. W. H. Felton preached. Getting old and unable to stand, he sat on a chair and preached for almost two hours one of his finest sermons to the largest crowd ever assembled under that tabernacle. No one seemed to get tired. The people were spellbound. Dr. Felton was a great preacher, a brilliant orator, and one of Bartow County's outstanding citizens of the day, as well as a member of Congress.

The Reverend Sam P. Jones, one of Bartow's famous sons and one of the most prominent preachers of his time, also preached here.

When the preacher came down out of the pulpit to call up mourners, men and women would go back in the congregation and urge sinners to go to the altar for prayer, while the congregation stood and sang some familiar song, such as, "Away over in the Promised Land," or "Mother's gone to Glory, and Don't You Want to Go?" All this time the preacher would be down one aisle and up the other, exhorting sinners to make preparation for death and judgment.

Back in the eighteen-nineties a revival was in progress at Cedar Creek Church, and many people were 'professing religion,' and joining the church. The doctor did not attend the services often, saying he did not have time. One day, during the third week of the meeting, I told him we were going to have company for dinner.

"Who?" he asked.

"The preacher and his wife," I replied.

The doctor scratched his head, and with a quizzical air, said, "Don't you know I have no time to fool around with preachers?"

The preacher and his wife came. After dinner the doctor and he went out on the porch. I don't know what they talked about, but after the guests left, I noticed the doctor seemed very serious. The next morning he picked up the baby, and taking the Bible from the reading table, went out on the road over a little hill to where there was a spring in a grove. When he returned he asked if I wanted to go to church that day. I said I did, and we went.

There was no preaching that day, just an experience meeting; men and women standing up and telling how God had saved them, and had been with them through the trials and temptations of life. One man said, "Brethren, I've been waiting for twenty years for my father to get out of my way so I could join the church, but I'm not waiting any longer."

The next moment the doctor was on his feet, saying "I am not going to be in my children's way. Lord, I'm coming home!" Starting up the aisle, the preacher met him with open arms. The people laughed, wept and rejoiced together, as people do whose hearts and souls are overflowing with the spirit of old-time religion.

The doctor joined the church, and was baptized the following Sunday. During the remainder of his life he believed in the old-time religion, and lived it every day in the week, every month of the year.

When I asked him why he took the baby with him to the spring that morning, he said "I thought it would make me more humble to have my little innocent child with me."

A short time before his death he said to me, "I am hungry to attend a good, old-fashioned revival meeting like we used to have at old Cedar Creek Church."

A few families owned a buggy, but a majority of the people did their riding in wagons. There were no paved roads, of course, only big roads winding through valleys and between hills. These were knee deep in dust during the summer, and knee deep in mud during the wet winter months when they were not frozen or covered with snow.

The dead were hauled to the graveyard in wagons. In those days, country people in Georgia never heard of a hearse. The dead were prepared for burial by some of the neighbors; washed, dressed, and laid out on two wide planks (the ends of which rested on chairs), and covered with a sheet. They were placed in coffins made by neighbors who possessed a smoothing plane, a handsaw, and a hammer. These coffins were covered on the outside with black cloth, inside with white cloth, and were just big enough to hold the body.

A long train of wagons would follow closely behind the coffin to the church, which would be packed with people. The congregation would sing several hymns. The preacher would begin the funeral sermon which generally lasted an hour if there was only one preacher; two hours if there were two. At the close of the service the lid would be removed from the coffin, and everybody in the church would pass by and look at the dead. Mothers even held their small children up to view the corpse.

Those old funerals could only be described by the word awful. They were hours long, and as nerve wracking as sobbing sympathy and rough-hewn eloquence could make them. The preacher exhausted his command of language and his physical strength driving home to the bereaved relatives the plain fact that they would find a vacant place and an empty chair when they returned to their home, and that never more would they see the departed on this earth, or in heaven if he had not been "saved" by becoming a church member.

Country churches had preaching services on Sunday in the month. Many folks walked to church. Some rode horseback. Occasionally a girl would be mounted behind her young man. The women rode with both feet on the same side of the horse, side-saddle. Any woman seen riding man style would have been everlastingly disgraced.

Truly, the church was the meeting house through which communities were held together, friend with friend.

VIII. COURTSHIP AND MARRIAGE

THE OLD-TIME GARDEN was a thing of variety as well as usefulness and beauty. The young people did much of their courting in these gardens.

One Sunday afternoon the young doctor and I took a stroll in ours. The walk through the garden was a little lower than the ground on either side. All around the fence grew raspberry vines, and, in their allotted places, horseradish, fever weed, sage, tansy, catnip, hoarhound, indigo, motherwort, calamus, and other herbs used in those days for the making of home remedies.

On the opposite side of the walk were bachelor buttons, old maids (zinnias), touch-me-nots, verbenas, marigolds, bluebottles, pinks, and other varieties of the old-time flowers. Herbs and flowers formed borders along the walk that ran through the center of the garden. Back of that grew all kinds of vegetables.

As the young doctor and I walked slowly along, he pointed to arrow of beets and asked, "What are those things?"

"Beets," I replied. "Don't you know beets when you see them?"

"I know I'd like to 'beat' Bob Banks," said he. That was the young man I was then keeping company with.

I wonder if all the mothers talk to their daughters as mine did to her girls. I can never forget what she said to me when I began to grow up.

"Now listen to me," she said, "You will be going with boys before long. They will make love to you, and try to kiss and pet you. Don't ever let them start anything like that. It may lead to your ruin, you must take care of yourself. No man is going to take care of you. His nature would not let him, if he wanted to. If he persists in petting, knock him down if you can, and he will respect you for it."

"It will be mighty nice if you can tell your husband that he is the only man who ever kissed you." I can truthfully say, that no other man, other than my husband ever kissed me. Yes, I married young, only seventeen, but I went with lots of boys, some of whom proposed marriage to me.

The doctor was twelve years older than I. He had been with many girls and was very popular with the young folks. He was of medium size, with black hair and moustache, dark eyes, low musical voice, and a magnetic personality. He was a shining light at all the dances and social functions. An experienced, cunning, wily, fascinating Romeo, while I was a very young, bashful girl unacquainted with the ways of the world.

After going with me about six months, he told me of his love for me. He said I was the only girl he ever loved enough to tie up with for life. He told me over and over how beautiful I was, how much he loved me, and that I was *different* from any other girl he knew.

When he asked me to be his very own little girl, I was overcome with happiness and excitement. I said, "Yes." When he gave me the engagement ring and put it on my finger, he said "Now let's seal it with a kiss." I replied, "No, no, I can't do that." With tears in my eyes, I said, "You know I love you better than anything on earth without that." "But we're engaged to be married," he argued. "You've proven everything to me except your love. If you loved me you'd want to kiss me." He was still holding my hand, his face coming nearer and nearer to mine. I turned my head and he pressed his lips to my cheek. I never meant to let him kiss me. What would Ma say!

I couldn't sleep that night. All night long I felt those silky moustaches on my cheek. I loved it but wouldn't acknowledge it, even to myself.

The next morning I asked Ma if it as all right to let your sweetheart kiss you *after* you were engaged. She replied, looking at my ring, "Sometimes one may, but it is safest not to."

I was in love with the doctor. I thought of him by day and dreamed of him by night. I was so happy I sang love ditties. One I remember was like this:

> Tomorrow I'll gather me roses,
> And twine them together in my long braided hair,
> And Richard will come in the evening.
> And smile when he sees me so fair.

One day I saw the doctor pass, riding old Bob. I had an idea he would stop on his return, so I put on a fresh print dress, powdered my face with "Swansdown,"[10] and waited for him. Sure enough he stopped. We sat in the parlor and talked. The weather was very warm, and he asked for a drink of water. I ran out and brought him a glassful. He drank about half of it, and sat the glass on the table.

Maybe I should not tell this. I've never told it before, even to the doctor. Of course it is silly, but it's gospel truth, and only shows how deeply I had fallen in love. Next morning I went to the parlor, saw the glass half full of water, and took a sip. It tasted so sweet that I called it to myself, "my sweetened water." Every day I went in there and took a sip, until I drank it all. Even now I remember that it was *sweet*.

My father's reaction to my engagement was not very romantic. It was getting to be an old story, as he had seven daughters, each one leaving home before they were twenty. I was barely seventeen, when the doctor asked for me. My father said, "D'you think you can support her?" The doctor assured him that he could. The doctor was not satisfied to settle down and be a country doctor. He and I talked it over, and planned for him to go to Texas, a nice town, start his practice, then come back to Georgia. He had his trunk packed, and ready to go.

---

[10] *Swansdown is a brand of flour.*

On the first Sunday in December, 1886, the biggest snow this country ever saw started falling. I was having a good time playing in the snow with my brother, and letting the large soft flakes fall on my cheeks. I like to feel the snowflakes on my cheek yet. It was piling up. I was not looking for the doctor, not in this snowstorm. But he came, on horseback, and couldn't get away.

The snow stopped falling on Monday, and measured on the level 26 inches deep. Drifts were ten to twenty feet deep. The doctor said, "I can't possibly get to the station, suppose we reverse our ideas and get married right away?" I said, "I'd like to think it over." He said, "You can get ready right away?" "Yes, I can get ready in about ten days I guess." As long as he lived, he teased me about "ten days." He forgot about urging, "right away."

My father went to Rome and bought my wedding trousseau, which consisted of a coat, hat, shoes, stockings (cotton, there was no other kind), and cloth enough for two dresses, a wedding and an infare[11] dress. The weather being bad, my father did my shopping for me and it was very satisfactory.

I felt like a well-dressed bride. And I was happy!

We did not have a big wedding, as my older sisters had. The doctor did not want it. He wanted to go quietly to the Baptist minister's home. So we did.

---

[11] *Infare - A reception, or party, given to a married couple.*

The next day we went to his father's for the infare, then after a big turkey dinner at his brother's in Adairsville, we returned to my father's. In those days the common bridal gifts to a girl were a cow from father, quilts and hens from mother, and of course a feather bed. You couldn't imagine a couple setting up housekeeping without these. The quilts were made of wool scraps. I had ten quilts. The doctor brought another feather bed and his trunk.

IX. EARLY MARRIED LIFE

WE RENTED a house in the village of Folsom. The doctor went to Cartersville and bought our furniture which consisted of two bedsteads, a dresser, four chairs and a large rocker. In the kitchen we had a stove, safe and table. We considered ourselves well fixed.

Sometimes things were pretty hard for us. The doctor couldn't collect enough to buy horse feed, so we'd have to go visiting his folks or mine 'til we could buy feed.

When we were married the doctor practiced medicine on horseback. His horse was claybank in color, named Bob. A singlefooter, with a right pert easy gait. Later he bought a two-wheeled cart. He would milk the cow while I cooked breakfast, so I could ride with him on his visits to patients all over the country.

We tried to keep a woman in the house so I could not be alone when the doctor was on night calls. We picked up a little Negro boy to feed the horse and cow, and bring in wood.

Josh was black as a crow, and always saying droll things. After he left, there being no one to stay with me, the doctor's parents came and lived with us for several years.

Sometimes the doctor would have calls eight or ten miles away. Folks living along the way would stop him to see some member of the family who was ailing. One day a man stopped him and said, "Doc, I want you to see Calline. She ain't been well fur a month. I think her liver's outen order."

Another time a woman ran out, waving her hands and saying in a loud voice, "Doc, stop! Johnny's bowels is runnin' off, an' I want somthin' fur him."

"Cut out the green apples and he'll be all right," the doctor replied. "If he doesn't get better, come to my house and I'll give him something." This family was always calling the doctor, but never paid.

In going about the country he encountered many dogs. Every country man had his dogs, mostly hounds. Some had squirrel dogs, fox hounds, and other varieties. Some were vicious and tried to bite. The doctor knocked them off with his saddle bags.

During these first years I read the doctor's medical books. The smattering knowledge I gained from them proved of great value in later years. I have helped him to set bones, dress wounds, and have administered anesthetics.

The doctor showed me all his most poisonous medicines, morphine, atropine, prussic acid, and tincture of opium, and mind you, there were no tablets; every powder was dosed out on the point of a knife.

He showed me the amount of atropine for a dose. One Sunday morning a man came and wanted some medicine for his wife. I don't know what "ailed" her, but the doctor went into the medicine closet. (This was in 1887, the second year we were married.) I went in, too. I always loved to watch him dose out medicine. "If that powder is a poison as you told me," I warned, "you are giving her too much."

"I don't think so," said he. " I think it will help her."

In about two hours the man was back, his eyes big as saucers.

"Doc, I want you to go see my wife as fast as you can get there! She can't see, she can't spit, and she can hardly talk."

"All right. All right. I'll go right now," said the doctor. When he arrived he found the woman even worse than her husband had described, but soon had her all right.

I could not help saying, "What did I tell you?"

"It's all right. It knocked her neuralgia high as a kite," he replied.

In 1894, we moved to Adairsville. There had been several robberies in town while we were living there, and the girl Maggie who was living with us, was of the nervous type. She was afraid when the doctor was away at night, so she and I generally sat up until he returned.

One night we were sitting up waiting for the doctor, and continued up after all the neighbor's lights had gone out. In the stillness that wrapped the outside world we could hear nothing but the chirping of crickets and the barking of a dog. We sat listening, expecting to catch the stealthy tread of feet outside of a window or the touch of a hand on a door, when suddenly we did hear footsteps. Someone was tiptoeing up that long back porch. I felt my hair begin to rise, and looking at Maggie saw she was scared almost white. We sat gazing at each other in silence for a few seconds. Then Maggie whispered, "A burglar!"

I nodded, and managed to ask if all the doors and windows were locked.

With bulging eyes, Maggie leaned towards me. "I hear him working at the back hall door. He'll get in and kill us!"

"Be quiet, and perhaps he'll go away," I replied in a whisper.

"Be quiet nothing! I'm scared to death, and getting scared worse all the time!" Maggie gasped.

Just then we heard the burglar tiptoeing back down the long porch, and after a few moments returning. We heard him pushing against the door.

Something had to be done. It would not do to just sit there paralyzed with fear until this murderous man forced the door open and entered the house. I grabbed the fire poker, saying as bravely as I could, in a voice quivering with fright, "I'll brain him with this if he comes into this house."

Maggie was crying hysterically now, but managed to say, "If you want to stand here and get killed, you can; but I'm going to call for help."

Maggie ran to the window, threw it up, and called weakly, "Help! Quick! Robbers!"

I grabbed her by the arm, crying, "For God's sake, don't call the Johnstons. There is no one there but the old lady and the girls. You'll scare them to death."

Maggie ran, expecting to be shot, and bravely, or rather desperately, opened another window and screamed, "Oh, Mr. Murphy, come quick! Robbers!"

Mr. Murphy lived across the street. Almost immediately we saw a light flash up in his house. In another minute he burst into our house, dressed in bathrobe and bedroom slippers, and grasping a loaded pistol.

"Now be careful, Mr. Murphy," I warned. "Don't let them shoot you. Be sure to shoot first."

"Where are they?" he demanded.

"At the back hall door," I whispered.

We all three moved silently toward the door. Carefully Mr. Murphy turned the key in the lock, opened the door, and there was the burglar bending over something. We could not see what.

Mr. Murphy fired. The burglar fell heavily on the floor. After a moment he began trying to get up. I knocked him over the head with the poker, and cried for Mr. Murphy to shoot again. I was so frightened and excited I was not conscious of what I was doing. But Mr. Murphy did not shoot. He had discovered the burglar was my pet calf.

X: WAITING FOR THE DOCTOR

TALES OF WOE

Don't tell me your tales of woe
As down life's road I go
It makes me tired, your woes to hear;
I do not sympathize, I fear.

My back is bent with a heavy load,
Of my own troubles, on this road;
If my way you want to cheer,
Let me see you smile, my dear.

Don't let me your burdens know,
By telling each and every woe,
My burdens will much lighter be,
When a smiling face I see.

WHAT TRIED my patience most was people, total strangers to me, coming to see the doctor and spending the day, waiting for him to come home. Many of them came miles. They were old patients, so of course it would have been an added hardship on them to return home and come back again. Nevertheless, it was an added task for me, having to make efforts to entertain them, and also prepare dinner for them.

Some of them would have toothaches. In those days the medical doctor was also the dentist. He did tooth pulling for his patients, carrying a pair of forceps in his saddlebags. At first the doctor had only one pair of forceps, universal, that would fit on any tooth; but he had so many teeth to pull that he bought a supply of pullers, one for each tooth, with gum lancet and elevator. I'll wager he pulled a bushel of teeth.

When a tooth had been aching for days or weeks and the pain could no longer be endured, the sufferer would either go to the doctor's home, or to the home of some neighbor where he had a patient, and the tooth would be pulled by sheer strength, after the doctor had cut around it with his pocketknife. Such dental surgery would be considered extremely dangerous now, but in those days I never heard of a person dying of blood poison as a result of having a tooth extracted.

Some of the people who waited for the doctor had rheumatism and would tell me about the different liniments they had rubbed on their limbs and joints without obtaining relief. Others would have some chronic ailment; and some, I suspected, had simply and excitable imagination.

On one occasion a man and his wife waited nearly all day. We had just bought a new piano on the installment plan. The woman asked me to play, so I began with "How Firm a Foundation Ye Saints of the Lord," when suddenly the woman began to sing in the sweetest voice I ever heard. I played on and on, just to hear her sing.

"You have a wonderful voice," I said.

"I used to go to all the singing schools and conventions and sing treble," she replied.

Another woman came one spring morning when I had my first mess of beans and potatoes from the garden, a big cobbler pie made of freshly picked dewberries, and new light-bread. A mighty good dinner, I thought. However, she did not seem satisfied. "You've got some mighty fine fryers. I ain't been well, ain't go no appetite at all. All I can think of that I could eat is chicken." When we went to the table, I poured her out a goblet of buttermilk. She drank it, then passed her glass back to me and said, "Ain't you got some sweet milk? Buttermilk swells me." She drank two goblets full of sweet milk and ate a big dinner.

Such things call for patience, and if this doctor's wife was not a patient soul, it was not because the circumstances of life did not teach her to cultivate that great virtue.

It was no unusual sight to see a wagon drive up with a man and his wife, half a dozen children, and a couple of hound dogs. All jumped out at once, except the mother who held a sick child on her lap, the object of the visit. The man would help the woman and baby out and they would come into the house. The children and dogs played around the wagon 'til the parents came out. Then they would load up and be off.

Sunday mornings gradually got to be like church at our house, with horses, buggies and wagons hitched around the doctor's office. People used to come and get medicine for themselves or some member of the family.

Sometimes the men would stay for hours, talking about the war. All the old people of that time were interested in their own and their neighbors' Civil War experiences. One old gentleman would always say the trouble with Sherman was the he was "too careless with fire."

I had my hands full with cooking, house cleaning and sewing. However, it was often necessary for me to care for patients who came for the doctor when he was away on calls.

One day a man brought his little boy who had swallowed a nail. I prescribed turnip greens and stewed fruit. The little fellow suffered no bad effects from either the nail or the remedy, and the father pronounced me a good doctor.

Another small boy had the habit of chewing paper wads in school and throwing them against the ceiling. One day he started to choke on his wads. The teacher tried to dislodge them by making him drink water, but it came back through his nose. Then she tried slapping the boy between the shoulders. When this failed she sent a big boy with him to the doctor.

I gave Robert some water, but it gushed out of his nose. Hardly knowing what I was doing, for it looked like the child would choke to death, I ran to the kitchen. I dished up a bowl of soft potatoes from a pot cooking on the stove, stirred butter in them, and told Robert to eat. The first few spoonfuls were hard for him to get down, but he kept swallowing potatoes until they dislodged the paper wad and carried it to his stomach.

"It was the best medicine I ever took," he told his teacher.

Sometimes patients from a distance would come to see the doctor, prepared to spend the night. They didn't want to go to bed at bedtime. They wanted to sit up and talked 'til twelve o'clock or later, telling about their pains and aches. It was exasperating.

One old hypochondriac always spent the day. He never tired telling of his "quare feelings, and pore appetite," and that lump in his stomach always "naggin'." The poor old fellow had a rattling cough, with all his other ailments. Every time he laughed or coughed it sounded like a pot boiling. He had been tiziky all his life. His skin was swarthy, he was very nervous, and took medicine all the time. He lived to be an old man.

I'm thinking of another family that always spent the day. They thought so much of us that they wanted to make a visit. For the life of me I couldn't see anything wrong with that woman. She grunted with every breath, except when she went to the table, then she ate like a working man. After dinner she resumed her grunting, which I am sure was a cultivated habit. I often thought, "Hell can have no terrors for the poor sinner who marries a saint or a grunter."

If the old-fashioned doctor could not do the patient any permanent good, in a physical sense, just talking, looking wise and sympathetic always had favorable results psychologically.

The doctors of today are too busy to stop and waste time in "convivial confab of nonsense." Not so with the old-fashioned country doctor. He was never too busy (thought he always was busy) to lay his hand on your shoulder and talk to you. He was really interested in everyone's welfare.

I recall another party who used to come in the long ago. They lived in an adjoining county and came periodically. The woman was going through the menopause. She was having hot flashes, wasting spells and palpitations of the heart. She wasn't satisfied unless she was taking medicine all the time. She was the kind of patient that was hard to please. She'd say, "Doc, you'll have to fix me something else. That medicine you gave me hurts my stomach, and didn't do me any good," or, "That last stuff tasted so bad it made me sick to look at the bottle."

"Mrs. Smith, you are going through the change of life, and you will have these uncomfortable spells. All women do. You must not get nervous over it. You'll soon be all right, and the way I see it, you don't need medicine," the doctor would assure her.

But she would whine and say, "That's what John says, but I know my feelings better than anyone else." Knowing the woman so well, the doctor, having tried every known remedy without any apparent benefit, resorted to a good-tasting harmless preparation consisting of a little bromide, a little simple syrup, flavored with a little essence of lavender. He knew her mind was sicker than her body, and told her, "If this does you any good, come back in about four weeks for a refill." Nature is a greater healer than doctors if given a chance.

Well, it acted like a charm. The woman returned at the appointed time, looking like a different person. "Doc, you have hit my case at last," she said. "That last medicine you fixed for me has done more good than anything yet. I believe it will cure me. I want another bottle."

Then there was the woman who brought her husband, and three bad children who meddled in everything, spilled my perfume and face powder, climbed the porch posts, and got into every kind of mischief. The doctor would come in about eleven o'clock, but it would take the man the balance of the day to tell of all his aches and pains. There was nothing for me to do but get in the kitchen and cook dinner for them. I'd run to the smokehouse and cut a piece of ham, run out to the dairy and get a can of beans, jar of berries, or some other fruit to make a big cobbler. We always had a hundred or more jars of fruit, jam, berries, peaches, pickles, preserves of all kinds, and jellies. Believe me we needed them. I never knew when we were going to have company.

Many times strange men and women, whom I had never seen before, would come, and wait to see the doctor, who would be away on calls. I would pray for the doctor to come before lunch times. My prayers were rarely ever answered.

An old Confederate soldier came ever so often and stayed as long as we would listen to his tales. He has lost his leg in the battle of Second Manassas, and could tell many hair-raising experiences in the war. He said the Rebel Yell was probably born at the battle of Chancellorsville, when the Yankees were retreating and Gen. Lee came on the field. It was the cry of victory, and stirred men's souls as nothing else on earth could.

The wounded and dying on the field of battle tried to rise from their beds of blood, they were so inspired. The sight of Gen. Lee or Gen. Jackson always inspired the Rebel Yell. Gen. Jackson said it was sweeter than music in his ear.

Job was right when he said, "Man that is born of woman is of few days and full of trouble, his flesh on him shall have pain, and his Spirit within him shall mourn."

So many old-timers came with their pains and aches, it seemed that the whole world was sick. They wanted relief, and so often no relief could be given, for it is "appointed unto all men to die."

XI: DREADED DISEASES

DIPTHERIA! The very word struck terror to my heart. When our three oldest children were small there was nothing to combat the dreaded disease. In the worst epidemic of diphtheria that I remember, seven children in one family had it, five of whom died. The family was very poor, and the children and parents were crowded into one room.

In another family two children were desperately sick. The doctor stayed with them, spraying their throats every few minutes. The little girl told her mother she was going to die, and divided her playthings among the other children. As she was dying she managed to whisper, "Mother, little brother has come for me,' and kissed the baby brother no one could see but herself.

When our youngest son was eight months old he had diphtheria. By this time anti-toxin was in use, so his father called Dr. McClain, at Calhoun, to bring some and a throat tube. He came with both, but as anti-toxin was something new, he did not administer enough. The baby was choking to death when they wrapped him in a blanket and inserted the tube into his throat. At first he struggled but at last began breathing more easily. The tube remained in his throat for five days; then Dr. McClain removed it. In a few hours he was choking again, and in great haste the tube was replaced. This time it was left in for seven days. After its removal he again began to choke. Once more the doctor replaced it, and it remained or six days more.

We were careful to keep the other children out of the room where the baby was. One day I slipped out while he was asleep to give some instructions about dinner. When I returned, there were the other children gathered around the cradle. When I asked what in the world they were doing there, they replied that they wanted to kiss little brother good-bye before he died.

Another dreaded disease was typhoid fever. Every year it claimed its victims. I remember one year the doctor had thirty-six typhoid patients at the same time, and they were scattered over a wide territory. During this epidemic he did not undress and go to bed for weeks at a time. He would come home, lie across the bed, and say to me, "wake me in three hours. I've got to go and see those patients."

He pronounced the typhoid of that year the most malignant he ever saw.

Six members of one family had typhoid during this terrible epidemic; the father, a grown son, and a daughter died. In another family two boys, aged sixteen and seventeen years, died and were buried in the same grave. An elderly woman was stricken, and said she knew she was going to die. The doctor answered, "You have faith in God, and trust in your doctor. Now, pull for the shore, and you will make it." She must have "pulled," for she recovered.

In those days everyone thought tuberculosis – they called it consumption – was hereditary and not contagious. I have actually seen tubercular patients sleep and eat with the whole family. In one family I knew well, six of them died of it. They did not think of isolating the sick ones, but slept and ate together, drank water out of the same dipper. One after the other died, until six of a big family passed away.

Tuberculosis was the most prevalent disease, and also the most deceptive. Patients never believed they had it.

A little lady near us had la grippe[12]; tuberculosis developed. She was stricken in the early spring, and lingered all summer, hoping she would get better. The truth was she was gradually growing worse. When the leaves began to fall she could hardly speak above a whisper. She had been organist at her church for years, and her husband was chorister. As he sat beside her bed, holding her little wasted hand in his, they sang together, she in a weak, breathless, broken voice, he with a tearful sob, "O, Come Angel Band. O, bear me away on your snowy white wings, to my immortal home."

She was soon borne to that home. Her daughter is now a missionary in war-torn China.

Millions have died of tuberculosis. It has perhaps taken the greatest toll of human life.

Pneumonia is the most common of the dreaded diseases. We've had several cases in our own family. Each winter of our married life the doctor treated many cases.

---

[12] *la grippe: influenza, the flu*

I can never forget one bad case, a young man in a very prominent family. The time for the crisis had come, the ninth day. The family was terrified. They would not let the doctor leave. The boy's fever registered 106. Even the doctor despaired of his life. When the fever went away he almost passed away. The doctor stayed beside him and did everything he possibly could to help him over the crisis.

The boy rallied and pulled through.

The happy father wanted the doctor to celebrate with him. He had some fine old rye. The doctor never could take more than three swallows of whiskey without getting sick. The man insisted that he take more, and it ended up with his taking too much. Being too sick (or drunk) to go home, he spent the night.

Next morning the sick boy seemed to be on the road to recovery. The doctor had another patient with pneumonia, so he left. This other patient was getting on fine. The mother asked the doctor to taste some fine brandy. The doctor took the bottle, lifted out the cork, smelled he contents, and commenced to vomiting. The lady said, "Now, look at that! He can't even stand the smell of liquor. He's my doctor from now on. He's not like old Dr. Dudley, drinking too much and getting drunk!"

The doctor laughed in his sleeve. The woman didn't know the reason for his sick spell. I've heard the doctor tell of it many times, and laugh. He knew his capacity for liquor and did not dare go beyond it. The last thirty years of his life he was a total abstainer.

Pernicious anemia is something to be dreaded. A man came in one day who actually frightened me. He looked as though he had lost every drop of blood in his body, as white and bleached was his face. Even his lips were pale, and his eyes looked like pearls. He waited to see the doctor, but no doctor could do him any good. He had pernicious anemia, and soon passed away.

I have seen so many sick folks, with so many different diseases that I've thought sometimes that the whole world was sick; very few people were in perfect physical condition.

There's cancer, another disease that is difficult to do anything with unless it is external and treated in its incipiency.

Haemophilia is an hereditary disease. Those affected are called "bleeders." The two cases I knew about died. It is transmitted through females.

Bright's disease is another fighting disease, and usually comes out winner. I remember some interesting cases the doctor had. A very prominent man, highly respected and much loved, was well advanced with Bright's the first time the doctor saw him. Mr. B. didn't realize he had kidney trouble. He thought it was his eyes. His sight was blurry and he could see two objects where there was but one. The doctor could not promise him a permanent cure, or much relief. The man was sick many months, and was getting worse, so the doctor suggested a prominent specialist be called from Atlanta. The specialist, unable to give any encouragement, told the patient Dr. Bradley was doing all that could be done. The doctor, not wanting to build up a big bill against Mr. B., told him, "I don't seem to be able to help you much, and there's no use my coming so often. I suggest that if, or when, you get to suffering, just let me know, and I'll come right over and relieve you." Mr. B. lived several months. The doctor was with him when the end came.

Another patient, Mrs. Dollman, was very sick with Bright's disease. The doctor was called, gave his favorite prescription, and she improved wonderfully. So much so, that she was able to be up and about, even visiting the neighbors. After about a year she began to go down again. The doctor told her family she could live but a short time. She was not a Christian and never went to church. Her folks, very anxious for her to become a Christian, asked the doctor to talk to her. He told them he was supposed to get folks well, and this was the preacher's job. But they insisted.

The doctor tried, but it was useless. He told them to send for a preacher. I think they did. Anyway, the woman died in a few days.

In those days a person was not permitted to die without being told the end was near, and the doctor was often compelled to break the sad news to the sick person.

The doctor took great pride in his profession. From what he collected for his services, he managed to keep buying medical books and journals. In this way he kept abreast of the times.

None of the doctors then knew much about that dread affliction which sends so many to hospitals for operations now days. I well remember when Governor William Y. Atkinson was operated on for appendicitis, the first such operation in Georgia. Also, I remember the first person to be operated on in our county. He was a patient of the doctor's. He is still living, a prominent minister of the Gospel. The doctor had many appendicitis patients, including three members of his own family.

Rheumatism was then, as it is now, a common trouble and hard to relieve. The doctor enjoyed giving the prescription that he heard a noted doctor (Dr. Osler) give at a national meeting of physicians. Here it is: "Go to an old maid who never wanted to marry, take her handkerchief, dip it in the pond of an honest miller, then spread it on the hedge of a preacher who never coveted anything that was his neighbor's, then take it to a lawyer who never robbed a client and get him to write his name across it, and next lay the handkerchief on the rheumatic limb of the patient. A sure cure is the result."

Doubtless all doctors had to deal with hysterical patients, the majority of whom are women. From my own experiences I learned just what a bad case of hysterics means to a patient, the doctor, and everybody concerned.

Germs and microbes are the subject of the shortest verse ever written:

> Adam
> Had 'em!

There have been germs always, but people did not know of them. I've seen mothers and fathers chew food for their babies, when they had rotten teeth in their own mouths. I've seen them take big bites of food and put it into the waiting mouths of their babies.

The doctor had only one case of hydrophobia. A young man from our neighborhood went to Texas. One night as he dismounted from his horse, something attacked him. He didn't know what it was, but thought it might have been a wolf. It bit him more than a dozen times. He consulted the doctor who advised him to go to Atlanta and take the Pasteur treatment. Instead he went to Atlanta and had a mad-stone applied. About two weeks later, starting to take a drink of water one morning, he went into violent convulsions that last two days. He became so violent that they tied him on the bed with ropes. He was so swollen that he did not look like a human being. Narcotics had no effect. Hundreds of people came many miles to see him, just out of curiosity. Mercifully, the poor man died.

The doctor has given the serum to quite a few people who had been bitten by mad dogs.

Scarlet fever was to be dreaded. Our oldest child had it, and we never knew where she got it. She broke out as red as flannel. The other children were with her, but none of them caught it.

Meningitis was the most fatal disease encountered. The doctor had many cases. A boy about sixteen years old was stricken one afternoon, and died in six hours. One of his sisters took it the day after he died and recovered.

Nerves! What is this thing they call nerves? Is it imaginary? Is it a symptom of a disease? What is it? It gives doctors more concern and trouble than any other disease. From the cabin in the pines to the palace of the prince, from the worker in the mills to the president of the large corporation, from the young schoolgirl and society queen to the octogenarian, none is free from nerves.

The rapid pace of present-day civilization and the highly competitive struggle for existence are responsible in great measure for the increased nervous tension of today and is, I believe, responsible for so many suicides.

The annual deaths in the United States from hypertension alone are estimated as one hundred and fifty thousand. Some regard nerves as a reflection on their intelligence, resenting any allusion to nerves. They feign other diseases, and deceive everybody except the family physician.

It is all in knowing how to control one's self. If a person has too much sympathy and attention, it will retard recovery indefinitely. The doctor must have the help of the patient and the co-operation of the family, in successfully treating the neurotic. I know whereof I speak. I've seen too many hysterical patients.

I don't hear much these days about cholera infantum; that used to be a dreaded disease of childhood. I've seen little fellows get sick and die in just a few days. Their stools had the odor of rotten wood, and were very watery. Usually brain complications set in and resulted in death.

XII: A FROLIC

O̲n̲e̲ ̲n̲i̲g̲h̲t̲ a man came and said, "Doc, Jack Small wants you at his house right away."

"What's the trouble?"

"I think there's going to be a 'frolic' there," the man replied.

Of course the doctor understood. Among the simple-minded hill people, the coming of a baby was generally referred to as a frolic.

In the early days of the 1850's a doctor could hardly be had at any price. Midwives had to be employed to wait on the women. Babies were born on someone's lap. If the husband was not very strong and became nervous, a neighbor was asked to do the favor. Just before the baby was to be born, the man sat down on a straight chair with knees flexed. The woman was placed with her back against his chest, her legs across his. The midwife was on a stool in front to catch the baby. The old expression, 'catch the baby' originated in this fashion. After the baby came, the mother was laid on the bed where she remained for nine days. Then she got up and went to work.

For the first few years after we were married I was very ignorant about the duties and work of a doctor's wife. There were so many babies born. All the poor folks had babies and more babies. The well-to-do's didn't have so many. I would listen to the doctor tell of these frolics, the gossip and jokes of the old women, 'til I got the idea it would be lots of fun to have a baby. We had been married for three years and no baby yet.

The doctor said he did not want me to have one; did not want me to suffer that much. I thought he was joking. How could it be so bad when other women kept having them? He couldn't fool me. No, sir-ee!

His cousin Jennie was going to be confined soon, and gave me a special invitation. I was thrilled, and could hardly wait.

Early one morning Cousin Tom came after the doctor, and said, "Jennie said for you to come too."

"I surely will," I answered, and soon we were there. Cousin Jennie was suffering some, about once every hour. Her face turned red and she squirmed around in her chair. I thought the baby would be born any minute. This was in the forenoon. She had only two women with her who said she would get worse at the turn o the day. Sure enough, after lunch she grew much worse. I never wanted to get away from any place so badly in all my life. I was sorry I had come. I was sick as a buzzard and getting very nervous.

As night came on, I was frightened out of my senses. Cousin Jennie was in great agony, and every time she had a pain I had one too. I called the doctor to one side and said, "Dear, let's go home. I'm scared to death. Cousin Jennie is going to die, and I am, too. I can't stand it another minute."

He answered in his low calm voice, "You should not have come if you feel that way. I think it will be over in about an hour. You must calm yourself. Get a grip on yourself."

"I can't," I wailed. "I'm suffering death myself. Do you reckon I'm going to have a baby, too? Every time she has a pain I have one."

I had given way to my feelings until I was suffering sympathetically. The doctor put me to bed, gave me a sedative to quiet me, and told me there was nothing wrong with me. So I lay there and took stock of myself. "I'm the biggest fool in Georgia," I thought. "There's nothing the matter with me. I must have a little self control." After lying there for a while, I got up and went back to the sick room. Cousin Jennie was suffering something horrible now, and in just a few minutes the baby was born, a ten-pound girl. Cousins Tom and Jennie passed away long ago, and the baby now lives in Washington, D.C. She will be fifty years old this September sixteenth.

After that experience I decided it would be no fun to have a baby and that I never, never would have one. Just one year later I went down through the shadow of death and became a mother. Believe me, I thought death would be a picnic compared to having a baby. After having eight, I haven't changed my mind.

The doctor brought more than five thousand babies into the world, and lost very few mothers or babies. Among those he delivered, some are now lawyers, judges, doctors, preachers, robbers, gangsters.

Pretty Boy Floyd, that young western desperado, was among the number. Pretty Boy had good, law-abiding parents and grandparents. He was born seven miles east of Adairsville. He was a fine, pretty baby, weight ten pounds. His beauty must have stayed with him through his life, as he was nationally known as Pretty Boy Floyd for whom the G men had a long hard hunt.

XIII: CASES

Woman
A woman can cook, a woman can sew,
A woman can dance and play;
But a woman shouldn't go to the field and work
For a woman ain't built that way.

Man
A man can plow and a man can hoe,
A man can dance and play;
But a man can't quiet a crying babe
For a man ain't built that way.

I WOULD advise every man to get married, for there's nothing like having a sweet little wife to take care of you and your money.

The only way for a man to argue with a woman is to keep silent.

Some old crank said, "After God made man He rested, but since creating woman neither God nor man has been able to rest."

Don't think every sad-eyed woman you meet on the street has loved, and lost. No indeed, she might have loved and got him.

An old-timer is one reared on a trundle bed.

One day I asked the doctor what was his most interesting case. He said, "I don't know. I have had so many, it is hard to say." For a little while he seemed to be thinking over the many cases he had throughout the years, and then said, "I remember one that I thought interesting at the time. A certain doctor was called to a woman who had been married several years. He diagnosed her trouble as being uterine fibroid tumor, and advised an operation at once. I was called in consultation, and asked to examine the patient. I told the doctor, who was also a surgeon, that I thought his patient was about four months pregnant."

"The doctor was sure she had a tumor, but said he would put off the operation for awhile. I told the woman's father that if she did not give birth within five months, I would return my fee, and stake my reputation as a physician upon the correctness of my diagnosis. In less than five months the baby was born."

The doctor was considered a fine diagnostician. A good surgeon in one of the best hospitals in this part of the state said he always felt safe in operating on the doctor's diagnosis.

Here are some cases I remember:

One day a man and his wife brought their son to the doctor. They said the boy had been puny a long time, and they believed he had a tapeworm. They said an old woman told them to make the boy go without food for a whole day, then have him throw his head back and open his mouth as wide as possible, meanwhile waving a piece of bread back and forth close to his mouth. They said they had followed the woman's instructions. The worm came up in sight, but, not having anything to pull it out with, they brought him to the doctor to pull out with his forceps.

Much amused, the doctor looked on while the prescribed performance was repeated. Back and forth the mother waved the piece of bread, while the father held the boy's head back. Suddenly the parents cried in unison, "There it comes, Doctor! Don't you see its big flat head?"

What they saw was the epiglotis. They were crestfallen when the doctor explained how serious it would have been had they succeeded in pulling out what they thought was worm in the boy's throat.

A man and his wife walked six miles to bring a baby to the doctor. It had a big hard lump on its hip. The skin was not broken, and the lump did not seem to be very sore. I held the baby while the doctor cut into the lump. The lance grated on something hard, and with a pair of forceps he pulled out a sewing needle.

A Mrs. Worthington came to see the doctor about a boil between her shoulders. He told her it was not a boil, but a full-grown carbuncle. At maturity it measured nine by twelve inches. The doctor thought she would die. She didn't lie down for weeks. It was so offensive one could hardly dress it. It was summer time, and creepers (maggots) got into it, which probably saved her life.

One night the doctor was called to deliver a woman. Her husband, stepping out in the yard, found the house was on fire. "O, my Lord!" cried the woman. "What shall we do? I can't be moved to another house. No one lives near."

The doctor told her to be quiet, and they would manage things all right. Dipping a bedspread and a sheet into a bucket of water, he threw them on the roof to the husband who quickly beat the fire out with them.

One indolent fellow, with a big family of course, lived about eight miles from our home in a cabin with a few patches cleared around it. One winter his children had whooping cough; some of them had pneumonia. The mother was so afraid they would take cold that she would not wash the floor where they had vomited. Going so often into this germ-filled house, the doctor caught whooping cough himself.

The doctor treated this family over a long period of years for every known disease, and never received a dollar for his services. They moved out of the woods up on a public road where they felt they were exposed to many more dangers, seeing so many people pass. They were frantic if one of their children got out of sight. One little boy named Pete thought it great fun to hide and see the excitement he created. Almost every day he played that trick, and the family alarmed the neighborhood. His sister would miss him; then all would join in the hunt, calling, "O, Pete! O, Petie! Ma, come quick! Lord God, Ma, Petie's lost! What will we do?" Everybody would be looking and calling, when Pete would crawl out of his hiding place, well satisfied with the hullabaloo he had caused.

When I was first married I was young and knew very little about a physician's duties. However, I soon learned. One day a very handsome young woman came to see the doctor. She looked healthy enough to me. The doctor looked at her tongue, felt her pulse, then began to thump her chest and back. Finally he pillowed his head on her billowy bosom and nuzzled around from one side to the other, then lay still for a long time. I thought it all unnecessary and was amused and about to be jealous. As soon as the woman was out of the house I asked, "Well, what on earth is the matter with that healthy-looking woman?"

The doctor looked at me with reproof in his eyes. "She has organic heart trouble, and is likely to die at any minute," he replied.

That was enough. I realized how foolish I had been, and vowed that no matter what happened, I would never be jealous or suspicious again, but trust my husband implicitly, which vow I faithfully kept for nearly three score years.

Perhaps thumb-sucking cannot properly be named a physical ailment, but it certainly can be a highly provoking habit. We once had a little Negro servant who was addicted to this habit. One day the doctor, in a hurry to start on a call, sent the Negro girl into another room for something he needed. She did not come back, and when he went after her, there she stood in a corner sucking her thumb. Irritated, he said, "Why don't you hunch, by gad?"

Soon after we were married, an old mountaineer came for the doctor. "Doc," he said, "I want you to see my leetle gal. She's mighty sick."

"What seems to be the matter?"

"I don't know. She's white around the mouth, and her breath smells awful bad. I think she's wormy."

"Does she vomit?"

"No. I don't think she does."

"Does she puke?"

The man's face brightened. "O, yes. She shore does puke."

The doctor went to see the little girl, and the father paid for the visit with a load of pine. But then, fat pine came in handy to kindle fires on cold mornings, and picking up pine knots in the woods was labor. So paying with pine was giving something useful.

Few nights passed that we did not hear the call, "Hello, Doc!" at the gate. Of course, there no telephones in those days. People had to go after the doctor. We heard the clop-clop-clop of a horse's hoofs on the road one night, and the familiar call. The doctor went to the door, and the man on horse said, "Doc, I want you to go see Paw. He's awful bad off, an' I can't git a doctor nowhar. I've rid all night, been to Calhoun and Adairsville, an' can't git nobody to go."

"Well, this is about the time I don't go either, when you can't get anyone else," the doctor answered.

The doctor would not go if he thought the sick person preferred some other doctor. He would not take another's patient unless the first doctor resigned, or had been dismissed. That was the way it used to be in the profession.

"But, Doc, Paw's about to dies," the man continued. "He's rale bad off. You'll sure git yore money, fur Paw gits a pension."

The sick man lived in an adjoining county, but "Doc" went.

A man in a covered wagon stopped at our house one day and said, "Doc, my boy out thar in the waggin's got the toothache. I ain't got no money, but I've a load of apples, an' if you'll pull the tooth, I'll give you a whole bushel of apples, or a quart of good 'corn[13].'"

The man and a big gangling boy came into the house, and the doctor opened his medicine case. At sight of forceps the boy jumped from the chair, gave one yell and knocked the forceps out of the doctor's hand. From the wagon he called back, "He can't pull my tooth, Paw. It 'ud hurt too bad."

The apple pies I had already envisioned on the table vanished with the covered wagon down the road.

---

[13] *Moonshine*

One day a man brought his wife to have a tooth extracted. The doctor, forceps in one hand, placed his hand around the woman to hold her head firmly against his breast. In another moment he had the forceps on the tooth, and pulled with all his might. The tooth came out, but could not be found anywhere. We instituted a search, but no tooth could be found. We had about decided it had dropped down her throat, when the doctor found it in his inside coat pocket; his attention being called to himself by a sudden severe pain in his side. An examination by another doctor showed that a rib had been broken when the tooth came out. For several days the doctor went about with adhesive straps on his side.

A Negro girl was brought by her grandmother to have an aching tooth pulled. After much persuasion and more scolding, she finally let the doctor get the forceps on the offending tooth. When it came out, she jumped from the chair, ran out of the house, and began going round and round, screaming, "Whar's I gwin?" "Yo'se gwine to de debble, dat's whar yo'se gwine," scolded the grandmother.

A little boy came after the doctor early one morning and said, "Doctor, Ma said for you to come to our house as soon as you can get there. Pa's bad off. He hollered all night. We couldn't sleep a wink fur him. Ma thought he was goin' up the creek several times."

The doctor found the poor man suffering intensely with angina pectoris. He lived but a short while. He went up the creek.

I remember two insane patients of the doctor's. One was about thirty-five years old, and the mother of five children. One Sunday morning the doctor was sent for. When he reached the house, several neighbors were trying to hold her on the bed. She had torn her clothes off and was kicking and screaming. The doctor took hold of her wrist to feel her pulse. In a flash she jerked his hand to her mouth and sank her teeth into it. The blood spurted, and the doctor told those present to pry her mouth open with a spoon. She held onto him like a bulldog. He finally broke her hold by twisting her ears.

He had the worst hand I ever saw. I was afraid it would become infected. It was a long time getting well, and left a big permanent scar. The woman was sent to the asylum, but soon came home. Then her husband died. She went crazy again and returned to the asylum for a year. Pronounced cured, she came home and bloomed out. She painted her cheeks, dressed herself up, and set all the old widowers a-flutter and running after her. It has been said that "when the devil goes fishing for men, he baits the hook with a pretty woman." She soon caught her man. He was a preacher. She lived with him five or six years. One day he sent after the doctor. When the doctor reached the house, he sat down in the living room. Mrs. Smith came through the door behind him and with her open hand slapped him on the back as hard as she could, exclaiming in a loud voice, "Hello, Doc. How are you?" The doctor jumped as though he had been shot – it was so sudden and unexpected. Of course she was crazy again, and had to be sent back to the asylum, where she died.

One day a man came and said, "I've got the hiccoughs. I've done everything I know to do, and everything the neighbors have suggested, but am getting worse all the time. I'm so weak I can hardly stand up." He was hiccoughing all the time he was talking, and seemed very much in need of medical aid.

"Well, what have you done?" the doctor asked.

"I've took nine swallows of water I don't know how many times," the man replied, "and my folks tried to scare me out of them. I've took sody, and a few snorts of whiskey, but nothin' ain't done no good. What is them things, anyway?"

"Hiccoughs is caused by a spasm of the diaphragm," said the doctor, giving him something to relieve them.

One day the doctor was called to see a man, and while holding the thermometer up to see if the mercury was standing at normal, said, "Now, open your mouth, Bill."

"Doc," Bill remonstrated, "you know I can't swallow that thing. You'll have to mash it up."

To a man having some kind of eye trouble, the doctor gave some powders. "There are two grains of this powder," he directed. "Put it in two tablespoons of water and drop a few drops in the eye twice a day."

"Well, but them grains will have to be mashed up, won't they, Doc?" the man inquired.

One night, back in his horseback days, the doctor was called to see a patient. It was a black night with a slow rain falling.

The messenger had a lantern, so they arrived at the patient's home without difficulty. On the return trip the doctor turned off the road into a trail which led through an old graveyard. It was so dark he could not see the trail, so gave rein to the horse, as he often did on such nights, knowing he would get home.

The horse kept the trail, and the doctor could tell by the deeper darkness when he entered the heavily timbered graveyard. When he was about half-way through it, his hat suddenly left his head. He dismounted and crawled around in the dense darkness 'til he found it, then got out of that graveyard as quickly as possible. He always afterward enjoyed telling this incident, and would say that knowing it was limb that had brushed the hat from his head did not keep him from feeling skittish and wanting the horse to step fast 'til he was out of that place.

I have seen little weakly women lord it over big strapping husbands in a way that was both amusing and disgusting. I remember one couple who used to come to see the doctor. They had about the worst boy I have ever seen, and all the time the mother would be saying, "John, go bring little Junior in the house before he gets hurt; John, Junior wants a drink of water; John, Junior will fall off that chair." Or changing her tune, "John, take off your hat; John, don't put your hat on the floor; John, bring me some water." John this and John that, and John something else; and John would jump like a jumping jack.

> "Man is a worm. He wiggles around 'til some old hen comes along and gobbles him up."

The doctor had his hands full treating all kinds of human afflictions, and taking care of surgical cases.

A certain judge's daughter went from our county to Atlanta. While there she stepped into a hole where a telephone pole had been taken up, and as a result of the fall was seriously injured. She came home, and her father sent for the doctor to examine her. He found she was injured permanently, and advised sueing the city for damages. Of course he had to be a witness in the case. After he had been in the witness chair a long time, during which the very able lawyer for the city did his best to break down his testimony, the lawyer asked, "Are you a gynecologist?"

"No," the doctor replied, "I am just an old-fashioned country doctor practicing medicine up in the hills of North Georgia. I've had my eyes almost scratched out by blackjack brush; and a doctor who has practices for forty years is supposed to know something about physical injuries."

The woman received satisfactory damages.

Once a fine old gentleman who was suffering with a disease of the bladder, and had been treated by several doctors without being helped, came to the doctor for treatment. Having recovered from the ailment, he sent his son to pay the bill. The doctor told him it was fifteen dollars. The son paid, and then said, "Thank you, doctor, for helping my father so much. He thought the bill would be a hundred dollars at least, and sent seventy-five to pay it."

I recall one occasion when the doctor was called to see a patient up in Dry Valley. A great many ponds of water were scattered around in this valley; the land was white rocky loam, very good productive land. Some of these ponds covered the "big road" for quite a distance. There had been a big rain, and the doctor could not tell just where the road lay. It was a real frosty morning. His horse had been over the road many times, and went along fine for a while. Suddenly the horse plunged down out of sight, the buggy followed, and the doctor found himself sitting in water up to his armpits. He pulled on the lines 'til old Nick came up, snorting and blowing water from his nostrils. The sudden plunge into that cold water chilled the doctor through and through. Fortunately, he was near his destination. Breakfast was almost ready when he entered the house, and the family gave him dry clothing and a hot breakfast. Then he prescribed for the patient, and was soon on his way home, not much the wear for his ducking.

Once two men rushed up to the gate at the same time. One was a well-to-do farmer who always paid his bills. The other a do-less-never-pay-anything kind of fellow. The first wanted the doctor to go to his house at once to see one of his children who, he thought, was taking pneumonia. The do-less man's child had been accidentally cut with an axe and, as he put it, was "bleeding to death."

The doctor decided the man who paid could get another doctor, whereas the man who didn't, could not. Like the Good Samaritan he was, he went to the aid of the bleeding child.

One day a man came and said, "Doc, my wife's been ailing a long time, and I've decided she has palography. I want you to give her something fur it."

If he is to be a successful physician, a doctor must know his patients as well as his books, and must learn the intricacies of human nature as well as the theory of medicine.

A man brought his little boy. He was very much excited and talked loud enough to be heard a village block. "I know I have more bad luck," he declared, "than any man alive. I paid fifty dollars last year for doctor bills, and now this young'un has gone and packed his ears full of beans, so I had to fetch him to you. I couldn't get 'em out."

While the doctor was preparing to remove the beans from the child's ears, I said, "I'm sorry for that poor man." The doctor replied, "Don't waste any of your sympathy. He does not mean to pay anything. That is his line." Sure enough, he never paid a penny for the treatment of the child.

A woman once came to the doctor about her left eye. It had been bothering her for some time, itching, burning, with a sensation as if something were crawling in it. Her eye was red and angry-looking. When the doctor examined it he found the trouble. There were little white worms deep down beneath the lower lid, very much alive, and about one-third of an inch long. He removed three of them, and her eye was soon well. She had no further trouble. Where did those worms come from, and how did they happen to get into her eye?

One day a woman about forty years of age came to consult the doctor. She seemed greatly worried about her condition. The doctor being absent, she told me her trouble. It was a habit generally associated with small children – bed wetting.

Being the wife and assistant of a country doctor, I learned the simplest details of people's lives. But the doctor's wife was one woman who realized the importance of not talking.

The doctor had a very sick patient, a boy about fifteen years old. Tom was drawn double with a terrible pain in the right side of his abdomen, vomiting incessantly, and with a temperature of 102. It couldn't be anything but appendicitis. The doctor explained the case to him and his parents, and advised an immediate operation. The father said he would take Tom to the hospital, but Tom was of a different opinion. "No," he cried. "God didn't put things in us for somebody to cut out, and I'll be d——d if they are going to cut me open."

I can't tell you how long that boy lay in bed. It was months. He wasted away to a mere skeleton. The doctor went to see him occasionally, but could give him only temporary relief. One day the father hurried in. "Doc," he said, "I want you to come and see Tom as fast as you can. He's been coughing constantly for a week. If he can't get any better, he's going to die right away."

The doctor said, "No, Tom's not going to die. He's too mean, lying there cussing all the time. I'll be right down and do what I can for him." When he got there Tom was having a violent spell of coughing. He suddenly commenced vomiting –

coughing at the same time – the most awful-smelling stuff. You could hardly stay in the room. It was pus. The doctor said nature must have walled off the diseased appendix. The pus had burrowed and worked its way on through the lungs, 'til he coughed it up. Tom got well. That was the only case of the kind the doctor ever had.

A man called the doctor. He was so excited he could hardly talk. Said he, "Tell the doctor to come as fast as he can. My child is awful sick. And tell him to bring his temperature and happydinktum (thermometer and hypodermic)."

A woman brought her child of about a year old. Said she, "This child ain't stopped screaming fur twenty-four hours, mighty nigh goes into spasms. I've walked the floor with her 'til I'm plum wore out."

The doctor prescribed a laxative, and in due time the child passed pieced of dishes, three buttons, and small rocks she had swallowed.

One year the doctor had a field of corn. The fodder was ready to pull, and he thought he could get a man who had long owed a bill to pull the fodder. The man agreed, but did not come near the field. A few weeks later he came to where the doctor was talking to a group of men and whined, "Doc, I've got a turrible headache. What's good fur it?"

"Pull fodder like hell," the doctor answered.

Once when the doctor was spending the night beside a desperately sick patient, he stared out to his buggy to get something he needed, and fell into an old well sixty feet deep. Some rotten planks over it broke when he stepped on them. As he plunged down feet foremost, he managed to catch with his feet and hands in the steps dug in the wall of the well, and hanging there, shouted for help. The men of the house heard him, pulled him out, and he returned to his patient.

Many times I've seen the doctor return with icicles hanging to his moustache and his ears almost frozen, in spite of the woolen scarf wrapped around his head. His feet were frozen in the stirrups 'til the ice would have to be knocked off before he could dismount.

In the practice of medicine a doctor finds out about the different dispositions of his patients. Some are the soul of kindness and love, while others are impatient, ill, and hateful. Some are appreciative of what is done for them; others are mean and not satisfied with anything.

I remember a case in particular, a boy almost grown, an only child, who had everything going his way at home. It seemed as though his father and mother were afraid of him. They obeyed him; instead of he, them. We'll call him Freddy. Well, Freddy came down with typhoid fever. He kept his poor mother exhausted from waiting on him. She was not allowed to sit down a minute. He cursed the doctor, saying, "You give me the d— dest medicine you've got. I'm not going to take it. It's not doing me any good." The doctor told him, "You can't cure typhoid fever in a few days. You'll have to be patient and take your medicine. You'll pull through." But Freddy said, "I'm getting tired of all this ballyhoo. When I get well I'm going to shoot you."

The doctor tried to have the parents call other doctor, but they refused. "No, we don't want anyone else. We have more confidence in you. Don't pay any attention to Freddy. He's just spoiled."

Freddy had double pneumonia later, and was a very good patient. He afterward grew up and made a good citizen.

I think parents are to blame, in a great part, for the way their children behave. If you don't rule your children, they will rule you. The Good Book says, "A child left to himself will bring his parents to shame."

As I look back over the years that have gone, I realize what a priceless blessing my strong body has been to me. A country doctor's wife and assistant during the past fifty years and more was certainly no job for a weakling.

During those years, many amusing and many pathetic things happened. Many things common in those days would be considered impossible now. Not many patients were sent from small towns and country neighborhoods to hospitals. Kitchen operations were common things, and many patients lived under circumstances that would mean certain death today. By kitchen operations is meant performing an operation on a patient stretched out on a dining table in the kitchen. I mean minor operations, such as amputation of fingers and toes, setting broken bones, dressing wounds, etc. No major operations were attempted in my kitchen. There were many such operations during the doctor's long years of practice. When a patient was carried to a hospital it was often in a two-horse wagon, over rough roads.

One such case seems incredible now. A woman had been suffering for some time with pains in the abdomen. The doctor found a great enlargement in the abdomen and advised an operation, as he was sure she had a tumor. The family kept putting it off because of the expense. The woman kept getting worse. At last they made up their minds to take her to a hospital in Rome, Georgia. She was hauled there in a wagon over roads that were rough and hilly. Part of the time she was screaming; part of the time she was half unconscious. However, she lived to reach the hospital, where the surgeon, Dr. Battey, removed a tumor that weight thirty pounds. The woman recovered.

There are all classes of people in the country, the same as in the city. We have the high, the middle and the lower classes. The share croppers, or renters, were good people, but they did not rate in society as did those owning plantations or substantial homes. The doctor waited on women of high class, when he and the nurse were the only ones present, perhaps the husband. He waited on others where there were six or eight women in attendance; these were the transients, moving into the community and out again swiftly.

The doctor was a plain-spoken man. Once, I recollect, a poor man engaged him to wait on his wife. He lived about twelve miles out in the country, and the doctor went as far as he could in his car. The man met him with a wagon and took him on to the home, that road being impassable by car.

The doctor was detained all night, so lay down to rest on their best bed, which was of straw. In the fall the man came to pay his bill of fifteen dollars.

"Doctor, I've brought your pay at last," said he, handing over the money.

"Tom," said the doctor, "since lying on your straw bed and feeling those hard slats push up against my back, I can't take your fifteen dollars. You need it worse than I do. You're an honest man. Keep the money." Tom insisted on his taking part of it anyway. I was present and heard the conversation.

"O, dear," said I, after the man left. "Why did you tell the poor man about his sorry bed. I'm afraid you hurt his feelings."

"I didn't mean to hurt him," replied the doctor, somewhat bewildered. "I was only telling him the truth."

Cases, cases, cases! I could fill pages with them, all different, just as life with a country doctor is different from day to day but to one who is interested in humanity, it is always fascination and worthwhile.

XIV: BILLS

ONE DAY shortly after we were married, I was looking through the doctor's account book and noticed, "John Smith" written above a long account, and underneath written, "Gone to Alabama." I turned a few pages and saw, "John Brown, " another long account, and written across it, "Gone to Texas." A few pages further on I came to "Jim Jones" and across his big account was written, "Gone to hell."

In this way the doctor had wiped these accounts from his book and out of his memory. Unpaid bills never kept him from answering the call of need and suffering.

In looking over his books at random, I found the following:

1885 – By one bushel potatoes, 60 cents.

1890 – By 300 bundles of fodder, $10.00

1896 – Charged off. Out of date, $25.00

1900 – One plow, $25.00

1902 – 300 bundles of fodder, $6.00

1902 – One bull, $18.00

1902 – By 52 bushels of wheat, $51.00

1903 – One pig, $4.00

1903 – By beef, $1.40

1903 – By 185 pound of pork, $14.80

1903 – By work, $5.00

1903 – By honey, $2.00

1903 – By two quilts, $3.00

1904 – By two gallons of syrup, $1.80

The quilts created quite a scandal. Gossips spread it around that the doctor was so hard about collecting his bills, he took the very quilts off a poor woman's bed for his pay. The truth was, having taken care of the family for a long time, the poor woman had no money and insisted on giving him these quilts. Much embarrassed, he took them. Refusing would have hurt the woman's feelings. They were not pretty quilts, and I soon gave one away. They served as a topic of conversation for some time, people taking sides for and against the doctor.

One man who owed a bill came to the house and said, "Doc, I'm having a hard time, but I want to pay my bill." He handed the doctor twenty dollars. The doctor said, "Now, Tom, if you really need this money, keep it now, and pay me some other time."

Tom kept the money, and some other time never came. I've always heard that money talks. I've learned what it says – "Goodbye."

One night a man hallooed at the gate. The doctor went to the door. "Doc, my wife's sick, and I want you to go see her. She wants you, too,' said the man.

"Where do you live?" asked the doctor.

"About six miles over in Gordon County."

"I'm awfully tired," said the doctor, "and I don't know you. You'd better get another doctor."

"I've got the money to pay you, and I want YOU," the man urged.

So the doctor went, and some time the next day the baby came. As the doctor was leaving, the man handed him seventy-five cents.

As a young doctor my husband dreamed of a coming time when he could locate in some city, where the practice of medicine was not such a rigorous task, and where financial rewards were greater. But the fact that he was destined to remain a country doctor never in the least degree dampened his spirit, or lessened his interest in his profession. All his life he remained a hard-working country doctor. A poor man, but a happy one. His patients were almost all poor people, and times were hard. In those first decades following the close of the Civil War there was very little money among the common people of Georgia. In many cases, even the smallest fees of the country doctor could not be collected.

Doubtless, if the old-time country preacher had kept books, they would have been very similar to those of the doctor. However, there is wealth greater than material wealth. The old-time country doctor and preacher laid up this greater treasure, where "thieves do not steal, nor moths corrupt."

Soon my husband's practice was extending in every direction; many calls coming from adjoining counties. Consequently he was on the road at all hours of the day and night. During these years consultation fees were five dollars, obstetrics five dollars, and ten and fifteen mile trips, two and three dollars.

Yet he was called upon to help build all churches and school house, and to contribute liberally to all fire and storm damages. Nothing of the kind was done in that part of the country were we lived there to which he did not contribute.

XV: PRENATAL IMPRESSIONS

THE DOCTORS of the present day do not believe babies can be marked in the prenatal stage of existence. I do believe they can. In fact, I know they can, because two of my own children were born marked.

One day a tottering old man came to see the doctor. His head was so bald it glistened in the sunlight. He had the palsy so badly he could not hold a glass of water to his mouth to drink. He was a fine old gentleman and had been a friend of the family for many years. When he asked me for a drink of water I brought it. He said, "You'll have to hold the dipper for me."

I held the dipper to his lips, and while he drank I gazed at his shiny, hairless head. Unconsciously, I scratched my own head above the left ear. When my baby was born she had a spot above her left ear as bald and shiny as old Mr. Collins' head. We did everything we knew to make hair grow on that spot, but not one single hair ever grew there. It is still bald.

Another of my children has a birth-mark connected with an accident that happened to a relative. A cousin of mine was shot through the thigh and the palm of his hand. He came to the doctor, who was away from home, making it necessary for me to give the boy first aid. I washed the blood off and bandaged his wounds. When my baby was born, he had no fingers on his left hand. I immediately recalled the fact that the boy to whom dered first aid was shot through that hand and at first thought his fingers had been shot off.

A newly married man went fishing one day and caught a big turtle which he carried home. Thinking to have some fun, he walked into the yard swing the turtle by the tail. His wife came out of the house, and he pretended to hurl the turtle at her. She ran, screaming, "Take that thing away!" He ran after her, swinging the turtle toward her. When the baby came its eyes were close to the top of its head, little beady turtle eyes, and it had almost no neck, its head fitting into its shoulders. Fortunately the baby died.

The doctor was called to see Mrs. Harper who was suffering from fright. She had walked out in the yard where a strange dog was growling. Thinking she could run it off, she picked up a stick, scolding at the same time. But instead of running away, the strange dog ran at her and reared up on her. When her baby was born it had one foot just like a dog's foot, round with short toes, and was crippled for life. It couldn't have been anything but the scare of that dog.

Another case of club feet in our community, a baby, was born to Mr. and Mrs. Jones. It had the worst club feet I ever saw. A neighboring woman who was pregnant went to see the sick woman and crippled baby, and, in turn, when her child was born it also had club feet.

XVI: ROMANCE AND TRAGEDY

*" 'Tis said of mother, maid and wife
That honor is a woman's life."*

DOUBTLESS, THE hardest thing the old-time country doctor had to face was a condition now and then arising in some highly respected family, a condition requiring the doctor to either sacrifice his moral convictions or refuse to bring his professional skill between such family and what seemed to be an intolerable disgrace. The doctor had to face this condition more than once during his many years of his practice. Never did he sacrifice his moral convictions. Such cases hurt him deeply. Always his sympathy for the family and the unfortunate girl was deep and sincere. But nothing could induce him to do what his conscience condemned as a crime.[14]

In the old days people were much harsher in their attitude toward such sorrowful mistakes than they are now. The girl who once brought such disgrace upon herself was disgraced for life. Of course such attitude was wholly unchristian, but it would have taken a brave soul to denounce it as such.

---

[14] *An abortion*

One such case will make clear the old-time doctor's standard; a standard from which very few of them departed, even when tempted with large sums of money.

The only daughter of a wealthy family was persuaded by her mother to discard the young man with whom she was desperately in love, and bestow her attentions upon what proved to be the wrong man.

The result was that one day the father of this unusually pretty girl came to see the doctor, telling him his daughter was sick. The doctor, suspecting the trouble, prescribed something harmless, and waited further developments.

It was not long before the father came back. This time he was greatly disturbed, swearing vengeance upon the man who had skipped the country and begging the doctor to save his girl and the family from life-long disgrace. The doctor told him that, while he was very sorry such a thing had happened, there was nothing he could do. To this the father said, "Just name the sum, and save my family from disgrace." The doctor repeated quietly there was nothing he could do. The family had to bear its unbearable burden.

The changed attitude of the public toward such cases is good, but the old-time doctor's unwavering loyalty to moral convictions is his crowning glory.

A beautiful young girl belonging to one of the best families grew up in our neighborhood. I will call her Serena Eldridge. She was little, slender and graceful, with blue eyes, light curly

138

hair. As Serena was the only daughter, with six brothers, the reader may know she was made much of by her parents and brothers.

One of these brothers was about the same age as the doctor. They had been close friends; going to parties and doing their courting together. Serena was very popular. Her brothers were devoted to her, guarding her with jealous care, nearly always taking her to social events with them. The time came when Serena met a young man of good family and grew very fond of him. There were no objections on the part of her family to his calling at her home, and soon people began to say, "Serena and Jerry are going to make a match." As girls have done since the beginning of time, Serena would dream of her handsome lover and their happy future together.

In the meantime, another close friend of the doctor was in Texas. While thinking of people and things back home in Georgia, he would think often of Serena. He decided to return, and if Serena were still single, and as beautiful as when he went away, ask her to marry him. Serena was single, and as beautiful, but from her own lips he learned her terrible secret, told when he asked her to marry him.

It was not long before the six brothers knew the secret. Armed to the teeth, they went on a manhunt for Jerry. He had left the county, but they found him and forced him to return and marry Serena. He left her in a few days and was never heard of again.

One dark night the doctor was called to the Eldridge home. He found Serena lying with a handkerchief over her face. The baby girl that came that night was an unwelcome addition to the proud Eldridge family. Unwelcome at first, but she soon became the idol of it, for she was a beautiful child and very intelligent.

Years later, when the awful epidemic of typhoid fever spread over the country, this child was one of its victims. She was then sixteen years of age.

When the doctor told the family the girl could not live, Serena cried, "O, doctor, I can't give her up. She is all I have. Don't let her die."

The doctor replied, "Serena, my arms are too short, and my ability too limited. I cannot do the impossible. Only God can save your child's life. She has passed beyond my reach."

The young girl died. Serena's brothers married and moved into homes of their own. Her parents died. She was left alone with her tragic memories.

One day the doctor was called to the home of a family whose head was a regular drinker. In the morning he always had to have an eye opener; for breakfast he would feel the need of an appetizer; after breakfast it was necessary to take a digester; between meals he needed a standby. On this particular day he had medicated himself heavily. He got his gun, whereupon the children badly frightened, hid themselves. His wife did not run. He pointed the gun at her and told her to dance. "You're not half dancing!" he yelled. "Get a move on yourself!" then he shot near her, doubtless to frighten her. She was dancing her best, but he was not satisfied and shot again, this time through the head, killing her. The children ran screaming to their grandfather's and told him what had happened. He called the doctor, but the poor woman was dead when he reached her. The man died in jail before the time was set for the trial.

One day in the spring of 1888 one of the wealthiest men in an adjoining county came to see the doctor. He was middle-aged, with iron-gray hair and moustache, and of the age psychologists call dangerous for men. He wanted the doctor to go and see the daughter of one of his tenants. He had been calling on this girl. Soon his wife would be home from Florida, and his son and two daughters home from college. The old donkey didn't want his highfalutin' family to be humiliated and embarrassed with an illegitimate child of his. The doctor was to examine the girl. If there was anything wrong, he was to send the girl and her folks back to the mountains where they came from. No one would be the wiser.

The doctor made the long trip. In finishing up the examination, he asked the girl's mother to bare Mirandy's breast to see if there was the circumscribed areola, which is one of the signs of pregnancy.

The mother refused. "No, I'll not do it. You can feel Mirandy's breasts, but you shore can't see 'em."

141

The doctor could tell the opulent Mr. Blank that the girl was all right. Sometimes, changing places and water causes a cessation of the menses, and gain in weight.

If some men knew themselves as well as others know them, they would be ashamed of the acquaintance.

A picture rises before my mind, that of a man who had lost his wife. A few days after her death, he came to our house and seemed heartbroken. After telling us how long they had lived together, what a good companion "Ma" had been, he burst into tears.

My mother said, "You have had a long and happy life, for which you should be thankful; besides, you must submit to the will of God."

"Yes, I know that," the old man replied, "but I'll never find another 'Ma.'"

Three weeks later he was married to a woman who lived on his farm.

This true story reminds me of another. A man's wife died, and he erected a handsome monument to her memory. On it he had this inscription cut: "The light of my life had gone out."

Within a few weeks he was married again, and decided the inscription on the monument would not look well to the second wife, he added, "But I have struck another match."

While we were living in Adairsville a very unusual thing happened. One Saturday night two Negro men came into town all excited. In walking to town they came close to Oothcaloga cemetery. They heard a strange noise, "Lak somebody a-cryin' right in de graves." They were so sure about it that some of the men went to investigate. The Negroes went with them to show the place where they heard that strange noise. Sure enough, they could hear the noise, but could see nothing. After searching for some time they located the weird sound as coming out of a newly made grave. There were some leaves on top of the grave. They raked them off, then a thin layer of dirt was removed. They discovered a baby girl, wrapped in a woman's petticoat. They brought the infant to town and laid her on the counter of a local drug store, where many people saw and marveled that she was found and her life saved. Some good woman gave clothing and food and kept the baby overnight. The next morning a local preacher took her to the Orphans' Home, at Decatur, where she thrived and grew to be a beautiful child, and was adopted by a wealthy family from another state.

It was reported that the mother had spent the day in the church, which was very near the cemetery. Several people recalled seeing a white face jerk back from the window, as they passed that day. She was a young girl who lived a few miles from Adairsville, and disappeared short after. The baby was named Dixie Adair, as she had been found near Adairsville.

One of the finest men I ever knew was left a widower with seven children. In a short time he married a woman with nine illegitimate children, and was a good father to them all.

One old gentleman, whose wife was a regular patient of the doctor, would get her to show him where she was in pain. When he came to see the doctor, he would press his hand down on the doctor's side and say, "Doc, my wife had a bad pain just about here; or maybe right here," moving his hand to still another place. "Yes, right here it was," moving his hand an inch or two to another place. "I want you to fix her up somethin' fur it."

When Reverend Lundy Harris, husband of the famous writer Corra Harris, took an overdose of poison, the doctor was sent for. He rushed into his office, got his stomach pump and antidotes. Just as he was starting for the patient, the Methodist preacher came and said he had just come from Mr. Harris' bedside, and that he was much better. So the doctor did not go. Mr. Harris died some time during the night. I've often thought if he had gone, maybe things would have been different.

Corra Harris built her home, "In the Valley," near the place of her husband's death. Part of the old original house is incorporated in the new building, which is of logs. The doctor had many patients in that house and community.

A young man in our neighborhood went up into the mountain section, from which his family had moved, and married his first sweetheart, a timid little girl of sixteen. His folks did not know he was going to get married 'til he brought the new addition to the family with the words, "Ye god, you'enses, this is my wife."

One day Caspar saw an old-time horse-drawn hearse pass the house and exclaimed, "Ye, god, what's thet goosey lookin' thing a-goin' yander?"

The doctor was often called into a home to settle family trouble, and by his skilful handling of the situation, would establish peace and retain the friendship of both sides.

Sad things and laughable things were always occurring. Life was always bordering on either the sublime or the ridiculous. The country doctor and his wife were always coming in contact with things unknown and un-thought of by other people. They knew all manner of family secrets; the tragedies of other people's lives were laid bare before their eyes. The country doctor's wife learned early the importance of not talking about such things, learned only because she was the doctor's wife.

The majority of people in those days lived a narrowly restricted life. Many of them were never twenty miles from their own front door. They knew nothing about the great world that lay beyond the line of hills that bounded their vision. Daily papers were unheard of; books were scarce; and those who could read, confined themselves to the Bible and a few religious books. Among such people it is no wonder that many things occurred that are hard to believe at the present day.

XVII: SUPERSTITIONS AND INCIDENTS

IN THOSE days there were many superstitions current among the people; beliefs that provoke a smile when they are recalled.

On one occasion when the doctor was called to deliver a patient, he noticed an axe with the sharp blade turned up under the bed. "What's the axe under the bed for?" he asked.

One old woman carefully explained the reason, and all in the room seemed surprised that a physician should need to ask such a question. It meant good luck for the patient.

Another common notion was that when exposed to measles the disease would not be contracted if the one exposed swallowed a buckshot each day for five days.

If a hoot owl was heard near a house, the fire shovel was placed in the fire to drive the owl away; its hooting in the vicinity was a sure sign of either sickness or death in the family.

To get rid of warts one had only to steal a neighbor's dishrag, rub the warts with it and bury it in some secret place. Warts could also be sold to another, or transferred to another person. They would disappear after being washed in stump water. Stump water was rain water that had fallen into a hollow stump. A buckeye carried in the pocket insured good luck.

The doctor had many operations delayed because the signs were not right, meaning signs of the zodiac. He found it useless to argue with the almanac-consulting folks. They had far more faith in that than they had in any man's new-fangled ideas.

One must stand erect when planning corn and beans, and stoop over when planting cucumber and melon seed. Otherwise one would have no luck with them.

A certain magical power was thought to reside in the number nine. To swallow nine sips of water was the common remedy for hiccoughs.

My cousin Frank had a sick cow and sent for the old Negro cow doctor who practiced in the neighborhood. The Negro looked the cow over and said, "Mr. Frank, if I was you I'd give her nine blades of fodder."

Whiskey was plentiful in those days, and the same curse it has always been. It could be bought in any amount, and the sight of drunken men on the public roads was nothing unusual. I have seen two men riding one horse at a mad gallop over the big road, yelling at the tops of their voices and firing pistols in the air. They were celebrating Christmas.

One young man who worked for the railroad company was sent to South Georgia for a job. He could not find a suitable place to board; but having to stay somewhere, he arranged for bed and board at Mr. Blank's. The first night there, Mrs. Bland said to her small son, "Johnny, get the jug and pass it to Mr. Doe first."

Johnny got the jug and passed it to Mr. Doe, and his mother said, "Mr. Doe, have some corn."

Mr. Doe, not being a drinking man, declined with thanks.

"Bring it here, Johnny," said Mrs. Blank. She turned it up and took a long drink, then Johnny took a drink and wiped his nose on his sleeve. "Go into the kitchen and get the dishrag and wipe your nose," ordered his mother. "I just can't stand *nastiness*."

When the doctor was graduated from medical college, he was given the cadaver *[of a deceased Negro]* he had dissected to bring home and string the bones together in their natural position. Before stringing, he had to strip them of the flesh. To do this he used his mother's washpot. The pot was filled with water, the "Negro" put in, and a fire was kindled underneath.

A neighbor came along, stopped and asked, "What are you cooking, Doc?"

The doctor replied, "I am trying to get the flesh off these bones so I can string them."

The neighbor got a whiff of the hot flesh, turned pale as a corpse, and said, "I've got to be going." He went in a hurry, and could have been trailed all along the way to his home by the vomit along the road.

In dealing with the public you meet up with all kinds of people, the selfish man, the stingy man, the liberal man, the honest man, the deceitful man. In fact, all classes of men.

Selfishness nowadays is called individualism, which is a nicer sounding word, but means just the same. So many of us are like the selfish man who prayed, "Lord, save me and my wife, my son John and his wife, us four, and no more."

We toil long and hard for self; educate self; beautify self; stuff self on the best the land affords; dress self up in the finest clothing money can buy. We make self happy. We live for self, we pray for self, we die for self.

This little verse illustrates the thought:

> I had a little tea party
> This afternoon at three
> And all the guests invited
> Were "I", "myself," and "me."
> 'Twas myself that ate the sandwiches
> While "I" drank up the tea,
> 'Twas also "I" who ate the pie,
> And passed the cake to "me."

The selfish, or stingy man is usually the one who pays as he goes. The lazy man is usually a poor man, and the poor pay as well.

We've all heard the story of the lazy man who would not provide a living for his family. His neighbors decided to bury him alive. One the way to the cemetery, one man's sympathy being roused, he offered the lazy man a bushel of corn. "Is the corn shelled?" asked the lazy man, lifting his head. "No, but it will be an easy matter for you to shell it yourself," he was told. "Just drive on your cart, brother," said the corpse, lying down again.

XVIII: OUR OWN FAMILY

WE WERE married almost four years before our first baby was born. We decided that there would no more children in our family, so named the baby after both of us. As the doctor was called "Doctor Dick," we decided to give her the name Dixie, spelling it Dicksie. My name, Ora, was added , making it Dicksie Orine. Old Dr. Dudley dropped in and laughed at us.

"You should not have given the baby your own name, doctor," he said. "There'll be a little boy along shortly, and he should have that."

We assured him there would be no more babies at our house. But in three years the little boy did come, as Dr. Dudley had predicted.

What a time we had with our first baby! She must have had the three months' colic that old women talk about. She cried day and night for six months. I did not know much about taking care of babies, even though I had come from a large family. I'd bathe her in the morning, fix her in her long white dress, and lay her on the bed, on top of the cover, where I could see her.

I missed the long drives with the doctor to see his patients and the leisure hours reading the doctor's text books. I had devoted lots of time to studying medicine. When his patients came and he examined them, I made out my diagnosis (to myself) and it was almost always the same as his.

Now life had changed.
I slept, and dreamed that life was beauty
I work, and found that life was duty.

One experience with Dicksie was really dreadful. I'd never been on a railroad train, so the doctor said we'd go over to Rome. There was to be a big celebration of something, maybe the North Georgia Fair. We set out early in the morning, drove to the station and boarded the train, Dicksie yelling to beat the band all the way. When we got off at Rome and started up Broad Street, the only way we could shut her mouth was to bounce her up and down. The doctor tossed her 'til his arms gave out, then turned her over to me. We couldn't enjoy anything, with that squalling child. My, but she had powerful lungs! I'm sure the town would have been willing to grant us a bonus to take that baby out of earshot.

The boy who was born three years after Dicksie we named Burton, after the doctor's father. He was a fine little fellow, and very welcome. Now, we thought, our family was just right, a girl and a boy. But we didn't know what to do about a bed for Dicksie. I had slept on a trundle bed, and so had the doctor. Almost all big families did the same to conserve room. You see, we could make up a trundle bed and roll it underneath our bed. She had never slept away from me and I knew she would not like it, but we decided to get the trundle bed. We rolled it up beside our bed, where I could be near her. Every night I held her hand until she went to sleep.

In two years another boy came. He was sweet, and we loved him dearly. Naming him for my father and a man we thought a great deal of, Honorable Charles F. Crisp, a Georgian, who was Speaker of the House of Representatives, we called him Crisp.

Two years later another little girl was born to us. I said, "What shall we name her?" The doctor took the Bible and went into the next room. I heard him say, "Eunice, Lois, Eunice, Lois." He came back, laid the Bible on the table, and said, "Her name is Lois."

"That's a pretty name," I agreed, "and it suits me."

Another two years, and another pretty girl arrived. We named her for the doctor's mother and one of my sisters, calling her Agnes.

The boy who came two years later was named Jefferson, after the doctor's younger brother.

When, two years later, the fourth boy arrived, I said, "This boy is going to be given his father's name, Richard." We added Gordon, which made a very pretty name.

The last child, a very pretty little girl, came two years later. We named her Lurlyne.

Somehow one's love never grows less, no matter how many children one has. It seemed as if we were carrying out the Bible injunction, to "multiply and replenish the earth." We had a houseful, and it was time to stop. I was about thirty-eight years old; we had four boys and four girls, all fine healthy children whom we idolized.

But I was weighted down with responsibility, and so was the doctor. We wanted to raise them to be honest, truthful Christians.

I felt responsible for the kind of citizens they would make, and if I were to die today, I'd still say, "I did the best I could." We sent them to Sunday School, and had them well educated. Now it is up to them.

The doctor, too, had a big responsibility. He had to provide food and clothing for his large family. It all meant work. We raised our own meat, chickens, garden vegetables, and kept one or two cows. We bought our sugar by the barrel, and I canned and dried all sorts of vegetables and fruit, made jellies and preserves, bought cheese by the hoop, and cloth by the bolt. I had a good sewing machine, so I made garments, cooked, churned and milked. I was so happy. It was all a labor of love.

Of course we had our Waterloos. Our children had the usual diseases of childhood, thrush, hives, roseola, measles, whooping cough. They all had whooping cough at the same time. When one coughed, they all coughed. Some of them were real sick with it. I had a time for about six weeks when measles struck. That was a heavy blow. Some of them had pneumonia with it, and we almost despaired of their lives. Diphtheria and scarlet fever were terrible, and we suffered great anxiety. Somehow we got through without losing any of them.

Dicksie started to school at the age of eight. Having been taught at home, she was ready for the third grade and led her class. One year later Paul started. He did well, too. They went to school for two years to the Reverend Gus Venable. He was a fine man and good teacher.

After Mr. Venable, Mr. L.T. Head taught the Folsom school for a number of years. I have always appreciated the fine work he did with my children.

As I've said before, it is a big responsibility to raise a large family. You will often be put on the spot by your own children. Mine have embarrassed me to the breaking point often.

I recall once, when Dicksie was about fifteen, while brushing her very long black hair, she said, "My head itches. I believe I'm lousy,' not noticing Lurlyne, the baby, standing beside her. At that time none of the children had ever seen a louse. A lady drove up to the front gate and Lurlyne ran to the door. When the lady asked for "Miss Dicksie," Lurlyne said, "No'm, she can't come out. Yes'm, she's here, but she can't come. She's lousy."

Our next school teacher was Miss Rainwater, a fine lady and a good teacher. Some folks moved into our community from away back, and sent their children to school. The first thing we knew, every child from twelve down, had his head full of lice. Miss Rainwater told the whole school to comb, and rub a little mercurial ointment into their hair. She said, "It's no disgrace to get lice in your head, but it is to keep them there."

When I found out my two youngest boys, Jeff and Dick, had them, I was almost frantic. I combed and combed, and looked and looked. I was so humiliated that I did it all at the back of the house. I would not have had anyone know for the world.

Sunday morning three or four men, one a stranger, were sitting on the front porch, when Jeff walked out with the newspaper in his hand. I thought nothing of it 'til he spread the paper down on the floor. I thought he was going to look at the funnies. Imagine my horror when he got down on his knees and began using a fine-tooth comb.

The men saw him and laughed. One of them said, "Let the boy alone. He knows his business."

One day the children were playing in the yard, when Crisp came in leading Dick. They were white as a sheet. I ran to them and demanded, "What on earth is the matter!"

"Dick has swallowed a June bug," faltered Crisp. That may sound funny, but it was far from that to me. I was exasperated, and did not know what to do. The bug might be a poison spider. The poor child was sick enough to die, and Crisp was scared stiff.

While I was wondering what to do, Dick began vomiting, and up came the June bug with every leg spread. It was dead. Investigating, I found out that Crisp was having lots of fun holding the bug by a string tied to its leg, and letting it tickle the other children's tongues. He said the bug pulled loosed from the string, and the last he saw of it, it was crawling down Dick's throat.

In raising a big family you never know what is going to happen next.

On the back porch one day I heard a commotion in the barn. I saw a cow suddenly appear in the upstairs doorway. It was a big barn, with a feed room on one side, and a stairway leading up from this room to the loft. The two older boys were looking up at the cow in nervous consternation. I found out that their uncle Bob's cow had gotten into our feed room and was eating our cow's feed. The boys closed the door and were beating the cow when she, frightened, ran up the narrow stairs into the loft. They had no idea she could be gotten down alive. If she jumped out of the barn door it would be certain death. They were two scared boys.

I told them to go tell their uncle Bob what they had done, and maybe he could rescue the cow. They ran and told him where his cow was, but I doubt if they told him how she got there. He brought her halter and went upstairs. With one of the boys behind the cow, he gave her a little tap with a switch. Soon he had old Cherry safe in her own grass lot.

The children had a pet kid that gave them much pleasure. They'd hitch it to a small wagon and take the baby for a ride. They taught the goat many tricks. If you crooked your finger at him, he would chase you. He was getting to be a big goat, when, one day, Agnes crooked her finger and he took after her. Billy chased her round and round, finally hanging his horns under the band of her dress and carrying her on his head for quite a distance. She screamed at the top of her voice, scared

157

almost to death. It was some time before the boys could rescue her. Old Billy was getting dangerous, so we had to send him away.

The doctor bought us a pretty new surrey, and a very gentle carriage mare. She was snow white. The children loved her like one of the family. We had such a good time driving around the country, to church and camp-meetings. Molly was safe for the children to ride and play with. One thing that aggravated them was that everybody in the settlement borrowed Molly to plow their gardens and patches. The doctor was so good natured he could not refuse.

We had a large barn, painted white. The children got some red paint and, in great big letters, painted on the side of the barn, "PLEASE STOP BORROWING MOLLY." It did no good. They kept on borrowing, but the letters stayed on the barn for twenty years.

We had a dog named Bogus. Bogus was just a puppy when Paul got him, but he was the worst pup I ever saw for dragging out and tearing things up. Bogus had a playhouse across the road, under a big oak tree, where he carried everything, and buried his choice bones. Whenever anything was missing we'd say, "Run out to Bogus' playhouse and see if you can find baby's dress," or shoes, or socks or anything. Once I was in a hurry to drive to town and couldn't find my new kid gloves. Sure enough, there they were in the playhouse.

Another thing which amuses me when I think of it. We took a little magazine called "Comfort." It is still published, though

I haven't seen a copy in ages. There used to be letters written to Comfort asking for advice on many subjects. Often I would read them to my oldest girl, who sometimes would not obey me. One day I said, "I'm going to write to Comfort and ask what to do with a bad little girl, and it will publish my letter all over the country, so everybody will know about it." I pretended I was writing the letter.

It acted like a charm. She was really good then. All I had to do was tell her, "I'll have to write to Comfort," and she would behave. I think that was better than punishing her. It also worked with the others.

When one has a large family one uses devious ways to control them. I wanted my children to be good (and they were good) without much chastising.

No two children are alike. Each has his own individual disposition, and a mind of his own. I found I had to deal with them in different ways.

Dicksie bought a new hat, all trimmed in ribbon and flowers. She kept it in a bandbox upstairs. Her cousin came one afternoon, and she took her upstairs to see the lovely new hat. Imagine her rage when she saw the floor literally covered with ribbon, flowers, and bits of lace. She was so mad, she vowed she'd kill that dog. But the boys kept him out of sight, until her anger cooled off.

On Paul's twelfth birthday, he received a gun from the doctor – which he had been long anticipating. He was so happy, he did not put it down all day, not even to eat, but held it across his lap while eating. That night I looked in on the boys, to make sure that they were all right, as all mothers do. There he lay fast asleep, with the gun hugged tight in his arms. I gently removed it and laid it on a chair beside his bed, where he could get it the first thing in the morning.

He and Crisp spent many happy hours hunting rabbits and squirrels. Bogus turned out to be a pretty good hunting dog.

For years I kept close to home, on account of the children, and, of course, someone had to be there in case a messenger came for the doctor.

Living as we did, eight miles from town, with the roads always hub-deep in mud during the winter months, we seldom went shopping during bad weather. Then, too, the country people seldom paid their doctor bills until along about Christmas; most of them waited 'til the last picking of cotton. But we were not left without warm winter clothes, even if we could not go after them. We had access to the largest department stores in New York and Chicago through their mammoth catalogues, which were certainly a blessing to country folks.

We could take a catalogue, go through every department and select each article we wanted. We appreciated these big catalogues, and the good warm sweaters, caps and shawls, heavy ribbed stockings, socks for the children and other wearing apparel. There were all kinds of toys, dolls, pistols and wagons, and games for the children. You could see right before your eyes what you wanted, and marked at very reasonable prices, too.

When the new fall and spring catalogues came, the old ones were not thrown away. No indeed, they were carried to the backy (later privy, now outdoor toilet) and placed on the seat. There, I do believe, they found their greatest usefulness.

Not many people in the country at that time had ever seen toilet paper.

I had so much to do that I didn't have time to teach the children their Sunday school lessons. I delegated Agnes to the task of teaching the two younger children their lessons. I remember the lesson one time was the GREAT COMMISSION, "Go ye into all the world and preach the gospel to every creature, beginning at Jerusalem, Judea, Samaria, and to the uttermost parts of the earth." She went over it time after time, but poor little Dick just couldn't grasp it. He couldn't, and he wouldn't try. She finally said, "Now I'm going to tell you one more time, and you've got to say it." He still looked dumb and helpless; she stamped her foot and demanded, "What is it?" He answered, "Go preach the gospel to Judy and Mary and everybody else." Really he answered better than he knew, for that was the Great Commission in a nutshell.

As a rule, people know very little about the Bible. I'm reminded of two men who were arguing about the Bible.

One said, "You don't know a thing about the Bible, you don't even know the Lord's Prayer."

"I do too," said the other one.

"Let me hear you say it then."

"Now I lay me down to sleep, I pray the Lord my soul to keep. If I should die before I wake, I pray the Lord my soul to take."

"Well, I didn't think you knew it, but you do," the other replied.

When I pass the old home, I think of the many happy days and pleasant hours we had there. My happiest days were spent there, with my children at my knees. I think too of the many trials and worries. But they drew us closer together, and after all that is life.

XIX: SICKNESS AND SORROW

IN OUR early days we remained in Adairsville only a few months. Then we moved to Calhoun.

During that summer there was a terrible epidemic of typhoid fever. Our little girl Dicksie was stricken and was desperately sick for weeks. Then I caught it.

From my bedroom window I could see the hearse passing, taking typhoid victims to the cemetery. It was not very encouraging for a typhoid patient. My father and mother, and the doctor's parents stayed with us. They nursed me and took care of the children. Finally it was decided to carry me to the home of my father, where I remained for six weeks.

When at last I began to improve I learned just what it means to be hungry. In those days typhoid patients were not give anything to eat, the idea being to starve the fever out. Doubtless, many patients starved to death before the typhoid did them in. One of the first things in the line of nourishment that was given to a convalescent patient was a little of the water in which a young squirrel or chicken had been boiled for nearly a day. My father went out and shot squirrels every day. Mother would dress them, put them in a pot of clear water, and boil and boil. I could smell it cooking, and hot water would come in my throat, my stomach would writhe and cry for food. At last the squirrel was ladled out, the water strained so as to be sure no tiny scrap of flesh remained, and a few spoonfuls of the water given me.

I begged and cried for just one taste of the squirrel flesh, but did not get it. To have swallowed one tiny scrap would have been certain death, according to the belief at that time.

After that siege of fever, the doctor's parents, my parents, and all of our friends begged and persuaded us to come back home to Folsom. With spirits low, ambitions dampened, and our finances below zero, we moved back. As the doctor always said when down and out, "Lick the flint and come again." That's just what we did. We stayed at Folsom and reared our family of eight children. That is where we spent our happiest days with our children, and with plenty of hard work.

A woman brought four children in the first stage of measles to the doctor. I had never had measles, and was pregnant. I had been told by old women that a pregnant woman never recovered from measles, and I was sure my time had come to depart this life.

I had measles, developing colitis first, and then a long drawn out case of hysteria. The children had measles, and some of them had pneumonia. How the doctor lived through that siege and retained his reason is still something that excites my wonder. I imagined my forehead was paralyzed, that a great tumor in my throat was choking me to death, and various other nonsensical things. I firmly believed that I was dying. After this state of affairs had existed for several weeks, the doctor changed his tactics. From being very sympathetic and patient with me he suddenly became indifferent and seemingly cruel. When I would tell him I was dying, he would say, "Well, let me see you die. You couldn't die if you wanted to."

I got so bad I could not bear to have him leave the house.

One night the father of a very sick child came for the doctor. I began to shake and begged him not to go. But he said, "I've got to make a living for you and the children." Seeing him come from the barn with his horse, I began crying out loud. I asked him to give me something that would kill me, as I was the most miserable creature on earth and I knew he no longer loved me. He turned the horse in the pasture and waited to see that sick child until morning. At last I realized that my condition was purely an imaginary one, and would ruin both myself and my husband if I allowed it to continue. I fought it like a demon and finally came out victor. I tell you a genuine case of hysterics is something awful.

When our youngest child was eight months old, she got hold of a green apple and ate part of it. She was taken violently ill. We did everything in our power for her, but nothing helped her. We gave all the patent baby-foods, formulas of cow's milk, preparations of sugar-of-milk, and every remedy that J. Lewis Smith[15] recommended for similar troubles. Sick all summer, she became so thin, her intestines could be plainly seen through the wall of her bowels. Her face became wrinkled

---

[15] *Dr. J. Lewis Smith was a prominent 19th Century physician whose medical treatment advice was published in various texts.*

like an old woman's. We had to nurse her on a pillow. A neighbor said to me, "I don't want to discourage you, Mrs. Bradley, but can't you see this child has no chance to live? The skin has grown down on the bones, there's no flesh between them.

One Sunday morning a woman from Pine Log came to see the doctor. He was not at home, so she came in to wait. I had just bathed the baby and laid her in the cradle. She was so exhausted she fell asleep.

Her toes and fingers were blued, her eyes half open. The lady looked at my baby and burst into tears. "The baby looks so much like a dead child it breaks my heart." Just imagine what it did to me!

Soon after that incident the baby began having convulsions. For a day and a night she was drawn in paroxysms. We had other doctors, and our closest friends were with us. I could stand it no longer. We went into the next room and waited for them to tell us it was all over. Imagine my surprise and happiness when my cousin ran in and said, "Cousin Ora, dry your tears. Your baby is better. The convulsions have stopped. She opened her eyes and knew her father." From then on she improved. The weather was getting cooler, and I'm sure that was in her favor. But it took a long time for her to gain back her flesh.

I can think of nothing more horrible than to see a little child in convulsions. I can close my eyes not and see that frightful picture; the little wasted form with limbs drawn in different positions, face contorted, one eye turned one way, the other rolling another way, screams every few minutes; two doctors holding the wrists where there was scarcely a thread of pulse. Only those who have gone through it can understand what I mean.

We had another horrible experience that same fall. Our oldest daughter was in the Women's College at Millidgeville. One afternoon I received a telephone message, "Your daughter is gravely ill with meningitis. Come at once." I almost dropped to the floor. Of course the doctor was out, but he soon came in. It was as great as shock to him as to me.

There was no possible way to reach Millidgeville except by train. We could not get one before the next morning at five o-clock. I walked the floor and prayed that she might live. We had eight miles to go to the Adairsville station for the train. In the meantime the doctor called Dr. Baird, a nerve specialist in Atlanta, who joined us on the train. I was so apprehensive. Meningitis! I knew it did its work quickly.

When we reached the college, two doctors and two nurses were with Dicksie. She was resting a little better, they told us.

When they telephoned us the afternoon before, they considered her in the jaws of death. Blisters had been applied the full length of her spine, and her poor, sick pretty head had been packed in ice.

I'm happy to report that she recovered. The doctor stayed with her for about two weeks. I had to come home to the other

167

children, whom we had scattered among our kin. When I arrived home I found all well except the baby, the one who had been so sick. She had pneumonia. I called the doctor, asked if he shouldn't come home, but he said, "Get my brother in Adairsville to see her. I can't come now. When I do, I'll bring Dicksie. Do the best you can."

Dicksie was partially paralyzed from that terrible disease, and could hardly walk for many months. In about two weeks we had a wire from the doctor, "Will be up on the eleven o'clock train Thursday."

I wondered how we could bring her out to Folsom. Everybody talked and had suggestions. Crisp said, and he was earnest about it, "Get Mr. Whitworth to bring her out in the hearse." There was no ambulance.

We got a neighbor who had a wagon with springs and a mattress, and brought her home. How thankful we were to all be at home again!

I've told these things just to show some of the fiery trials we had in rearing our family. We had other serious illnesses, such as the typhoid fever Jeff had at the age of nine, the colitis Lois had at two years that lasted three weeks, and numerous other ills that threatened their lives.

I have tasted all the different phases of life, and like the Apostle Paul, I know how to "abound," and also how to "be abased." I've been on the mountain top and down in the valley of Baca, suffering as much as possible in this world.

And that is life.

MADRIGAL

When the sun's first golden rays
Fall gently on the rose,
And the mocking bird sings sweetly,
And the cock-a-doodle crows,
I raise my weary eyelids;
And look out on the morn,
And on God's ways I meditate,
For another day is born.
And shall there be another day?
The great God only knows,
We sow and reap, and laugh and weep,
Then fall asleep,
And vanish – as the rose.

XX: MOTHER

A Tribute to My Mother

Who tucked me in my trundle bed –
Who laid her soft hand on my head –
Who taught me to pray at even' –
Who pointed me the way to heaven?
'Twas no one else but mother.
Of all the names, there is no other
Quite so sweet to me, as "mother."

For the soothing touch of her gentle hands,
No one, like a mother, understands,
The precious words she so often said
Are memory's jewels, on a golden thread.
I'll cherish her memory, as no other.
For one can take the place of mother,
My precious darling mother.

MY MOTHER was a great help to us in raising our children. When one of them became ill, we went after Ma. Just her presence, not to mention her many kind acts, seemed to lift our depressed spirits and give us courage. Many times at midnight the doctor went after her when one of the children had high fever or was restless and jumpy.

Don't be alarmed," she would assure us. "This child is going to be better soon." We would be looking for the worst, but she always cheered us by declaring all would be better by morning.

My mother was so calm and quiet, never excited. I owe everything I am, or hope to be, to her. I find myself many times, even now, craving to see my mother; wishing she could come to see me, to stay with me a while as she used to do. I have so many things I'd love to talk over with her.

When I was a child I thought Ma could save me from all the ills of life. In times of storm, with lightning flashing, thunder roaring and the wind lifting big trees out of the ground, if I could get near my mother, I would be safe.

Even in my dreams I thought Ma was a sure refuge. I can never forget one dream I had when I was about twelve years old. We lived on a hill, and down the slope was the barn. I dreamed I was down at the barn milking the cows, and had finished and started to the house. I looked toward the south and saw smoke boiling up. I stopped and gazed in wonder and horror. The smoke seemed to be getting nearer and nearer. As far as I could see, there was black smoke, turning red with fire that was sweeping everything before it with an awful roaring sound. I was frightened to death, and began running. If I could only get to mother she would save me. I ran and ran, but could not make much progress. (You know how it is in dreams.) When I reached the house I felt the hot flames in my face, fell to the ground – and woke up. I thought the end of the world was coming.

In 1880 there was a prediction that the end of the world was coming in 1881. Everybody was talking about it. I remember reading in the papers something like this:

> "The world to an end shall come,
> In eighteen hundred and eighty-one."
> - Mother Shipton[16]

I guess that accounted for my dream.

When my mother "went away," a great light went out of my life. I was in a hospital recovering from a major operation when she died.

I can truthfully say that the doctor loved his mother-in-law as if she were his own mother.

As I said before, both my mother and father were a great help in rearing our children. They enjoyed having them with them, and of course spoiled them.

My father was not able to work then, he had grown so stout, weighing three hundred pounds. He had a gentle buggy horse named Daisy. The colored man Mack would hitch her up to the

---

[16] *Mother Shipton was an English "soothsayer" in the 1500's. A posthumously published book appeared in 1641 with prophecies attributed to Shipton. In 1862, a Charles Hindley republished the book and falsely added this "prophecy."*

buggy and Pa would ride over the country and to the creek to fish.

Our fourth child, Lois, was to last to stay with them, and how she did enjoy those rides! She got the idea that she didn't want to mind her grandmother, and Ma, knowing the great pleasure Lois took in going places, would say to her, not wanting to force obedience, "All right. One of these days I'm going to die, and you shan't go to my funeral." Lois would yell and cry, then do what she had been told.

My sister Lalla was my nearest neighbor during the first years of our married life, and was also a great help to me during those trying times when we were both rearing our children. Her's and mine grew up like brothers and sisters. Their names were Ruth, Howell, Naomi, Bill and Jack. Ruth was put on a committee to raise money for foreign missions when she was ten. She went out to her father's store where a crowd of men had congregated, and asked each one for a contribution, and getting none, she stamped her foot and said, "No, you won't give me any money, and them little heathens is dyin' and going to Hell, every day."

CARRIAGES

Carriages without horses shall go,
And accidents fill the world with woe.
Around the world thoughts shall fly
In the twinkling of an eye.
The world upside down shall be
And gold be found at the root of a tree.
Through hills man shall ride,
And no horse be at his side.
Under water men shall walk,
Shall ride, shall sleep, shall talk.
In the air men shall be seen,
In white, in black, in green;
Iron in the water shall float,
As easily as a wooden boat.
Gold shall be found and shown
In a land that's now not known.
Fire and water shall wonders do,
England shall at last admit a foe.
The world to an end shall come,
In eighteen hundred and eighty one."

XXI: POLITICS

THE DOCTOR was always interested in politics. He was very hospitable, inviting his friends from the city to make our house their headquarters. Consequently, election day was a busy one for me.

I remember on one election day a certain candidate's workers were our guests, two young city men, good looking and very dignified. A young lady was visiting my daughter, and we five were at the table, when the little son I had delegated to sit beside the cradle and keep the baby quiet, appeared at the door and shouted, "Mamma, I can't do a thing with that old baby. He wants his titty." The trouble with Crisp was that he had eaten up his piece of chicken and biscuit and was wanting more.

Always the comic and tragic were being mixed in a manner that made life a constantly changing thing.

Turning from medicine to politics, it does not seem that people take the interest in politics and elections they used to. When I was a child and Felton and Lester were running for Congress, the people were so deeply interested that they would have fought for their favorite candidate.

The doctor and I went to a barbecue in Adairsville once, and there was such a crowd we almost had to fight our way to the table. What oratory the people were treated to, before and after the meal was served! No such oratory is heard these days, nor such enthusiasm as was manifested then.

It was at this barbecue that I saw my first buns. When we had finally pushed our way to the table, the doctor asked me what would I have. I said I would take some of those big biscuits. Years passed before he ceased laughing at me about those big biscuits. At that time there were a great many things in the world that country and small town people had never seen. On elections days, folks came to the polls in throngs; came walking through the valleys and between the hills, across woods and fields, came riding in two-horse wagons, muleback and horseback. The scattered country gentry came in cumbersome buggies.

Of course only the men voted, hence election day was strictly a man's day. The voters stayed all day at the polls, chewed tobacco, smoking corn-cob pipes, swapping yarns, exchanging views on things in general.

Arguments were common, often leading to fist fights, loud threats, cursing, and raising Cain generally, especially after a few visits to the fence corner or brushpile where the jug was hidden.

Nowadays we don't have long-winded speeches, like we used to have. Then politicians would speak for half a day at a time. Though sometimes they cut it down to two or three hours.

We are living in a fast day, speeches and sermons must be brief. Like a woman's dress, just long enough to cover the subject and short enough to be interesting.

I always prepared dinner for company on election days. Sometimes the doctor would be there, but more often he would be away on calls. Many times I've dressed to go to church or some public gathering, when the doctor would get a last minute call and I would have to undress and stay at home.

The doctor's hospitality extended to preachers, traveling salesmen, politicians and strangers passing through. The preachers always made our home their stopping place, on meeting days and during revival meetings.

The doctor was very progressive. We had the first telephone in that part of the country, the second automobile in the county, and the first Delco lighting system.

XXII: TRANSPORTATION

THE DOCTOR began his practice by riding old Bob, a claybank horse, and many miles he travelled that way.

The first vehicle we ever owned was a two-wheeled cart, of which we were very proud. I got a great thrill out of riding over the rough roads with the doctor, bouncing up and down as we went. No one was ever prouder of a fine limousine.

Then it was a buggy, and it so much more comfortable. The tired doctor took long naps on the road. One day a woman's scream awoke him, and there was a child under the horse's feet. The woman kept screaming with all her might. The child had on a red dress, and the doctor, thinking it was blood, was frightened almost as badly as the woman, until he found the child was unhurt.

Another time he went to sleep while riding over a narrow road with a deep ditch on either side. He met a woman walking, and she, seeing him nodding from side to side, thought he was drunk. Just as he came upon her, he woke up and snatched the lines that had fallen out of his hands. The woman fell into the ditch, and the doctor had to help her out.

When the doctor was going anywhere on the train, he always hurried to be on time, even if it necessitated getting up before daybreak.

He said no countryman ever got left. If he had to catch a train he was going to be there before time. It was the city fellow who got left.

But it was the automobile that made the greatest change in our mode of transportation, although Molly and the surrey had been a real joy.

Of course we had read about automobiles and seen pictures of them in the papers. We laughed when we thought how funny one would look running along the road without a horse. We hope to live long enough to see one, but did not actually hope ever to ride in one. However, it was not long before they began to pass along our country roads and frighten the horses nearly to death. Soon afterward the doctor bought one of the first in our county.

Talk about excitement! When that little red Maxwell arrived, it took the doctor to turn the wheel, Paul to use the brake, and little Crisp to blow the horn! The roads had been somewhat improved, so we could use our little red car in summer when they were dry and free from deep holes. But we had lots of trouble with that car. Sometimes it would run, more often it would not. Sometimes the doctor would start off in it, and it would "sull" on him. He would have to be brought back in a buggy. Then he would send someone to tow the car in and get a mechanic to work on it. At that time no one seemed to know enough about the mechanism of an automobile to be much help, when for some reason it acted up.

Still, the world had moved a long way from the time when a young man took his best girl to church and parties on horseback, the girl dressed in a long riding skirt buttoned up the side. Sometimes she would ride her own horse, and sometimes be mounted behind him, riding sideways, of course.

We had to keep a horse, just the same.

Our four sons, as they grew up, took over the job of chauffeur. First Paul, until he went off to college; then Crisp, 'til he, too, went away to school. Then Jeff, and lastly, Dick, drove the succession of cars we owned. They all adored their father; but they did not trust his driving. "Papa gets to studying about his patients," they'd say, "and is apt to run the car into a ditch, like as not."

Let the telephone ring in the middle of the night, and a sleepy kid would come down the stairs pulling on his clothes, ready to drive his father anywhere, over rough mountain roads, through the dark woods, and ofttimes past neighborhoods as rough as the roads. Then sit, perhaps for hours, sleeping if he could, while the doctor went inside some farmhouse or cabin to deliver a baby, work over a pneumonia case, or other desperately sick patient.

Sometimes it meant rushing an emergency case to the hospital in Rome, twenty or thirty miles away. Once Jeff made a record run there with a child that was choking to death with a bean in its throat. The child was saved.

Yet in all the years I never heard one of the boys utter a grumbling word about doing this service.

Other cars of other makes followed our little red one. Two were stolen, stripped of every removable part.

One night, the doctor had parked in front of the large Dalton hotel and gone inside to read a paper before the Whitfield County Medical Association, of which he was president. He came out late in the evening to find the door handle had been smashed, his overcoat (a Christmas gift from the children) stolen, and worse still, his bag of surgical instruments that were worth more than a hundred and fifty dollars, all gone!

Years later, with a son and a son-in-law each piloting his own plane, the doctor was game enough to make flights with them, to see how Georgia looked from the air. I took one flight.

XXIII: WORLD WAR

Knit, Knit, Knit
For Freedom's cause,
our soldier boys are loyal,
brave and true.
And Uncle Sam needs every one,
his duty now to do,
To win this war we've got to work,
we want to do our bit.
And that is just the reason
that we knit, knit, knit.

We're knitting on street cars,
we're knitting on the trains,
We're knitting when the sun shines,
we're knitting when it rains,
And when we go to meeting,
and in the pews we sit,
We take our knitting with us,
and knit, knit, knit.

If you're loyal to your country,
and want to do your bit,
Take up your yarn and needles,
and I'll teach you how to knit.
Wrap the thread around your finger,
push the needle through;

Throw your thread around, like this,

O that's the way to do.
Until the war is ended,
O yes we'll do our bit.
Just listen to our needles sing
KNITTITY, KNITTITY, KNIT.

As I sat by the window, my needles clicking in and out of the yarn, knitting sweaters and socks, caps and mufflers for my two boys in the service and for the Red Cross, the above verses flashed in my mind.

The World War was raging, the net was spread from Maine to California, and the flower of America's young manhood was caught in it. Every parent's heart was filled with fear and apprehension.

Our two oldest sons volunteered in 1917. Paul, the eldest, a young doctor just finished with his education and starting a practice of his own, became a Lieutenant in the medical corps of the Army. Crisp was a pharmacist and entered the medical department of the Navy.

My two oldest daughters were married; Dick and Lurlyne were in high school. With so much going and coming over bad roads to the railroad station to bring them home and carry them back, we had moved from Folsom to Adairsville. Being right at the station made it easier for all, especially the doctor who now had a drug store handy.

Paul, after intensive training in different camps, sailed for France some time in August 1917, and was stationed at Field Hospital Number 148 near Bordeaux.

Crisp was given special training in bacteriology, and made a number of trips across the Atlantic Ocean on the U.S.S. Siboney.

Paul was worked to death. The Spanish influenza broke out in the overseas army. No. 148 was filled with patients, and more were coming in. Several doctors were taken down, placing extra duty on the others. Paul had no rest day or night. He contracted the disease, and with the complication of bronchio-pneumonia, lived only a few days. He passed away on October 16, 1918.

We looked for a letter from him, as he was always good about writing. The doctor met every train, but there was no letter. On November the fourteenth we received the official telegram telling of his death, one month after it happened. I don't know any words that can describe the awfulness and tragedy of that message. The doctor was prostrated, and had to give up his practice for a while. Paul's commission as Captain was also a month too late.

Crisp was on the high seas during much of his service, and we feared for him all the time. He was on his first brief furlough when the news came of Paul's passing. It was a help to us all to be together.

Once when the Siboney was at Bordeaux, Crisp obtained leave to go ashore and visit the grave of his beloved brother. He said no one could know his feelings as he stood beside the grave of the brother he had adored and who had adored him. They were inseparable in their childhood and young manhood. What one knew, the other knew. Their love for each other "surpassed the love of women."

Cruel war! The breaker up of homes and happy hearts!

I remember during this time we were limited to a certain amount of flour. I made biscuits with two parts meal and one part flour when this order went into effect.

We had a good friend, a well-to-do farmer, who raised plenty of wheat and everything else needed on his farm, and had no boys in the service.

This friend came and said, "I don't want my old family doctor to eat corn bread. I have plenty of wheat, and I'll be only too glad to furnish you with all the flour you need."

"That is very kind of you," the doctor said, "but you don't understand. If my country wants me to eat corn bread in order that my two boys, with all the other men in the service, may have biscuits, I am more than glad to eat corn bread. I appreciate your kind offer but I can't accept it."

During the World War many people hid things, and profiteered on them. That was not the spirit of true Americans, the stock that made this country what it is.

188

Two years later, on November 11th, Armistice Day, our son's body was brought back home and lovingly placed in the Adairsville cemetery.

We just couldn't leave him over there. He had loved his home too well. Though it seemed like a second death when the flag-draped casket with its escort of soldiers entered our home, we felt that it was best.

Relatives and friends gathered about us, offering sympathy and comfort. There were quantities of flowers, and an impressive service as we laid him away.

Now, there's a little overseas trunk in a corner in a back room. Sometimes I go in there and softly raise the lid (it's like raising the lid of a casket) and gently lift out an officer's uniform. I place the empty sleeves around my shoulders, bury my face on the empty bosom, and pour my heart out in tears, thinking of the time when his strong arms and manly young form filled it perfectly.

The doctor and I suffered together and comforted each other in our great sorrow, as we walked softly down through the valley of Baca which the Psalmist calls the "Valley of Weeping."

I have always thought that the World War was an unjust war, and that America should never have entered into it.

I love my country, but I love my boys better. I feel sure that every Gold Star mother feels the same. Protect our own country, yes! George Washington was right. We should avoid all foreign entanglements.

My Memory Pictures

(Dedicated to my eldest son, Burton Paul Bradley,
lost in France, Oct. 16, '18)

While the rain is gently falling,
And my eyes are wet with tears,
I wander back o'er time's dim way
To dream of days of yesteryears.

Hanging on the walls of memory,
Looking straight into my eyes,
Are my loved ones, long departed,
Happy now in Paradise.

First I see is dear Grandfather,
Straight and firm and full of grace,
In full uniform and saber,
Strong, commanding kind of face.

How I loved his big brass buttons,
As I sat upon his knee;
And played with tassels on his shoulders,
While he told war tales to me.

Next is Grandmother, so gentle,
Hair like snow and cap of lace;
Sorrow, trouble, days of weeping,
Left its imprint on her face.

Next comes Father, great and noble,
Good and kind and patient, he,
Like the brilliant clouds at sunset,
Linger briefly, gloriously, leaving only a memory.

Mother comes next, in the long row of pictures;
I almost hear her gentle voice,
As she used to sing sweet lullabys
That made my heart rejoice.

Speak softly, tread lightly, for this one most precious,
Is the last one in the row,
So young, so strong, so handsome,
O What makes my heart ache so?

I seem to hear his gentle voice,
And feel his warm embrace
While gazing into those eyes so true,
And on his noble face.

O Memory, sad Memory,
Sometimes I would forget,
When it stabs my heart like a dagger
And my eyes with tears are wet.

Always seeking, never finding,
Golden memories, sacred things,
Perishable as evening shadows,
Out of the heart, like tiny fluttering wings.

Like a broken and empty chrysalis;
The beautiful butterfly gone,
An icy hand clutches at my heart,
O Memory, but I must carry on.

Across the silence of the shadowy years
Come golden memories, and silent tears,
My departed loved ones, come into my dreams,
And glide upon my memory, like shadows o'er streams.

XXIV: GOLDEN WEDDING

As December 1936 drew near, the children said we ought to celebrate our golden wedding. The doctor, too, was enthusiastic over having a party, so I consented. Dicksie's house was selected for the event, as it was larger than ours, and we made our plans.

No formal invitations were issued. We had so many kinsfolk, and the doctor's acquaintanceship was so wide, somebody might be overlooked and be hurt. We just sent a little notice to the newspapers in the counties where we had lived, stating that "Doctor and Mrs. R.S. Bradley will keep open house on the afternoon of December 18th to celebrate their golden wedding. No gifts, please." Well, that great day came, and so did all the family, the children, in-laws, and all the grandchildren. All looked real nice.

The doctor had a new suit. I fixed his tie just right and brushed his hair – he was not bald like most men his age, but had a nice crop of soft white hair. The silky black moustache was now close-cropped and gray. He looked the fine gentleman he always was.

I, too, was dressed up in a handsome dark blue velvet dress.

Evidently friends thought than no gifts did not include flowers. Messengers came with baskets, boxes, and bouquets of the most beautiful flowers. They covered all the rooms lavishly, and their perfume filled the whole house. I never dreamed so many lovely large yellow blooms cold be found at that season. There was also a stack of letters, suitable cards, and messages. We felt overwhelmed.

But the weather acted up. It began pouring raining before daybreak, and continued 'til after nightfall, with a cold wind blowing. Our spirits began to droop about noon. We thought all our preparations and refreshments would be wasted. The doctor was as disappointed as a child. He thought nobody would venture out in such weather, quite forgetting the many miles he had ridden on old Bob in storms as bad.

Just as we had given up, the door bell rang, and kept on ringing, 'til after five o'clock. It was after dark before the last car left the house. Many had driven forty or fifty miles to reach us.

They came from half a dozen towns, and farms in four counties. The bride's book showed more than three hundred and fifty names. The old friends, the new friends, the dear friends, the kinsfolk, came to offer congratulations and best wishes to the old-fashioned country doctor and his wife.

XXV: EVENING OF LIFE

Autumn

In Autumn when all nature dies,
and leaves turn red and gold,
And the full ripe grain is garnered,
let me Thy face behold,

My work on earth will then be done,
I'll ask a servant's place
To serve Him with eternity,
who saved me by His grace.

When chilling winds sigh deeply,
and the last rose petals blow,
I think I'll hear my loved ones calling,
dear Lord, then let me go.

WE HAD talked much and looked forward to the time when the doctor could retire from the hard work and responsibility of the practice of medicine, and sit down at home to enjoy the evening of life. It seemed that we had never had much time together. He was always so busy, and I was not idle. So we moved to Dalton to be near our children where we were not known, and where it would not be so hard for him to retire. But that was where we were wrong. It was not long until it seemed that every person in Dalton knew him. He found himself answering calls and practicing medicine day and night. Our long looked for rest never came.

An all-wise Providence ordered it otherwise. Even after he fell and broke his hip, people came from far and near to see him and ask his advice. Always a friendly soul, the doctor soon made a host of friends. He was a regular visitor at Stone's barber shop, and they enjoyed his jokes and quick repartee. He thought a great deal of the all the doctors of Dalton, they were just grand to him. I shall never forget their kindness. Also I must mention Dr. Robinson, of Chattanooga, who operated on his hip and saved him so much suffering. I must mention our pastor. He was a great source of joy and pleasure with his frequent visits. He always came in with a smile and a friendly greeting, not with a long face and a "Hark from the Tomb a Doleful Sound" look, like so many preachers take into the sick room, as though they had come to bid you the "last farewell."

Our pastor made many visits to the doctor's bedside, and these visits were always bright, encouraging, cheerful and uplifting. After the doctor passed away, I was thinking on these things, and these lines are the result.

WHAT I LIKE BEST ABOUT MY PASTOR

>What do I like best about my pastor?
>He walks each day with the Master.
>His gentle voice, his smiling face,
>His tender touch and saintly grace,
>   I see in him, a faith so true

The Master's face is shining through.
That's what I like about my pastor,

He grows each day more like the Master.
He is not rich in silver and gold,
He has treasures in heaven of riches untold.
Christ lives in him and I can see,
The lowly One of Gallilee.
The sick and burdened are soothed and cheered
By his kindly deeds and comforting words.
I pray God bless my humble pastor,
And keep him always, like the Master.

The doctor was able to be out in his rolling chair in the fall when the Seventh District Medical Association met in Dalton, a short time before he passed away.

He said to me, "I believe I'll get Buford (his nurse) to roll me over there. I have always liked to attend these meetings."

"The meeting is going to be upstairs in the City Hall, and Buford couldn't possibly get you there. There's no elevator in the building. He might let you fall and cripple you all over again."

"Don't you reckon some of the doctors will come to see me?" he asked.

"Yes, of course they will," I assured him.

He had Buford bathe him and put on a fresh shirt. Then he began to watch, expecting some of the doctors to come. He knew them all. In a little while Dr. Joe P. Bowdoin came in, put his arm around him, and said "Dick, I'm so glad to see you I'm going to hug you." The doctor cried with pleasure, and they had a good visit together. It was "Dick" and "Joe" all the time. Dr. Joe had come up on the train for the meeting, and I appreciated his visit more than he will ever know. The doctor watched all the rest of the afternoon, and kept saying, "I know some of the others will come after the meeting is over."

"Don't expect them, dear," I said. "Doubtless they have patients to see after they go back home, and they'll be in a hurry." I tried to excuse them so he would not be so disappointed. About seven o'clock he said, "Turn on the front porch light, so they'll see it and stop by on their way home." I turned on the light, then sat down and cried, and I'm crying now, thinking of it. I could not bear to have him so disappointed. He lay there, looked and listened, just like a little child. At last, tired, worn and grieved, he fell asleep.

I turned off the light and thought to myself, those doctors were all fine, good men, and would gladly have come in and spoken a few words to the poor, crippled, worn out doctor who had spent his life in the practice of medicine, and loved the profession so much. They just did not think how much it would mean to him.

XXVI: LOOKING BACKWARD

IN THE more than fifty years that I was the wife and helpmate of an old-time country doctor, I learned of life in all its phases. I drank from its overflowing cup of happiness. I learned the weight of its burdens, the keenness of its pain, the depths of its sorrow, the joys of its triumphs, and the sting of its defeats. I learned the greatness of work honestly done, and the nobility of unselfish service rendered others. I learned how devastating is ignorance of the great laws of nature, and how certainly suffering follows the violation of these laws.

During these years I mothered my own eight children, watched beside the cradle in which lay my own sick baby, felt to the full a mother's anxiety when a child was away from home and dangerously sick, and drank of the cup of suffering that only those mothers have drained who have had a boy in the full glory of young manhood die, with the ocean tossing its hoary billows between him and her arms.

During those years I witnessed much of human suffering, learned much of the limitations and privations that marred and maimed the lives of others. I helped the doctor with many an operation in our own home, and many times administered ether while my baby cried or played or slept in another room of the house.

Those were glorious years of love, of devotion, of duty, and of happiness, and through them all I could never to the full realize the nobility of the man heaven had given me for a husband. Nobility clothed him like a garment. Service was the watchword of his life. Love for all God's children was the ruling passion of his life, and to walk through the years at his side, his companion, his helpmate, was the high privilege granted me.

> "I know not where his islands lift
> their fronded palms in air.
> I only know I cannot drift
> beyond His love and care."

A little while we have been separated; but we shall meet again, just inside the shining walls of that City whose Maker and Builder is God.

In writing this book I have done so spontaneously, just as it came to me from the recess of past memories. I had in mind only the purpose of leaving to our children a brief record of their father's life, that they might have the inspiration of his idealism and example to encourage theme and give them cheer in their own undertakings and trials. I have touched only a few of the high spots in this humble man's more than half a hundred years of active practice as a country doctor in the hill section of North Georgia.

I began writing about six months before the doctor's death, and consulted him about many things, and many of his experiences. I have not enlarged upon anything. Now, as his life has closed, I close my book.

Having walked with him, worked with him, and slept at his side for more than fifty years, I think I know the greatness of his nature and the idealism that was the controlling power of his life.

On the 26th day of April, 1937, the doctor fell and broke his hip. Though he had the best of treatment from the finest surgeons in this section and was weeks in the best hospitals, the bones did not set. For the last eighteen months of his life he was an invalid; but always a cheerful, sweet-tempered invalid who still intensely loved people, and wanted to serve those in need.

> Sunshine and shadows have mingled
> in the year that has passed away.
> Sunshine and shadow will mingle
> in the year that I meet today.

It was hard to realize he would return no more. It was hard to believe that the flash had gone out of his dark eyes, the chuckle of his throat. But as I look around me at the pile of letters and telegrams, and the throng of sad-faced friends, the fragrant flowers heaped upon his grave, I realized I must walk alone the few remaining miles of this earthly journey. Yet I will not walk alone, for a precious memory will accompany me, and that Divine Friend in Whom he placed his trust.

In all his busy life, whenever he had a call, he was in a hurry to fill it. When the last Call came, he was in a hurry to go – so true to his life and habit. The Call came just as he would have had it. On Monday he sat on the front porch, and waved at people passing. Tuesday he was not feeling so well. Wednesday he was better, and full of the old cheerfulness until about noon. At ten o'clock he had written his last prescription; written it for his little grandson. At three o'clock he passed away with a heart attack.

Many beautiful tributes were paid the doctor by people who knew and loved him. Among the papers these tributes appeared in were the Dalton Citizen, Dalton News, Cartersville News-Tribune, Bartow Herald, Calhoun Times, Atlanta Journal, Chattanooga Times, State Medical Journal and the Emory Alumnus.

Following are some of those tributes:

"With the death in Dalton Wednesday of Dr. R. S. Bradley, those who practice medicine in North Georgia lost one of the most respected and illustrious members of their ranks, and mankind lost one of its most benevolent friends.

"The world needs more citizens who in passing at the age of eighty-one, with fifty-five years of service to humanity to their credit, could observe,

'I was glad to have helped'".

Taken from Tribune News, Cartersville, Ga.

TRIBUTE

"When the roster of world heroes is completed, all the names thereon will not be those of warriors, but high on the list will be the doctors who, headed by the Great Physician, have throughout the ages gone day and night, Summer and Winter, to minister to suffering humanity. Among those benefactors we may be sure appears the name of Doctor Richard Smith Bradley who answered his last Call from his home in Dalton, Georgia, Wednesday P.M., October 19, 1938.

Clipping from the Bartow Herald

TRIBUTE

"DOCTOR BRADLEY AS I KNEW HIM

By a Lifelong Friend"

"Doctor Dick lived in and near Adairsville all his life except for the past twelve years that he made his home in Dalton. Fifty of those years I knew him well.

In the fifty-three years of his active practice, he never had a diagnosis reversed. He was sympathetic and generous; never knowing how to say, "No." Having endurance, riding over mountains and valleys, night and day, rain or shine, hot or cold, my friend was an inspiration to me."

TRIBUTE

"By Another Lifelong Friend"

"There lies the whitest man that ever lived. I've seen him drive old Celum when his buggy wheels were solid ice, in sleet, rain, and snow, and his lines frozen in his hands, and the poor devils wouldn't pay him."

TRIBUTE

"By Jessie Baxter Smith

In Dalton Citizen"

"In his life, his character, and his achievements, Doctor Richard S. Bradley was the perfect answer to the question, 'What is success?'

In such a man the potential greatness of humanity is revealed, and manhood in its beauty and majesty is manifested. Because such men live and labor among us, we know that what gives them to us by making them possible, is an Eternal Reality that shall not pass away, and our own faith and hope grow stronger, and our own vision of the Everlasting grows clearer. Beside the bier of such a man, in the deeps of our souls we can cry out with the inspired Apostle, 'Oh, Death where is thy sting? Oh, Grave where is thy victory?'"

TRIBUTE

By the Reverend J. L. Clegg

Pastor of the First Baptist Church of Dalton

"He was a loyal husband and devoted father. His was a beautiful family life, and the devoted wife and the seven surviving children rise up to call him blessed; but above all, he was a Christian Gentleman.

There was a deep undercurrent of religious faith in his life. He was a lovable character. His was a rich and full life. He will be greatly missed by his legions of friends.

Precious in the sight of God is the death of His saints.

May the Father's richest blessings abide upon all who mourn his going."

In the days when Doctor Bradley was still practicing medicine, and in leisure hours could be seen walking with his boyish swing up and down the streets of Dalton, talking to men, women, and children, his face wearing its merry smile, and his blue eyes a-twinkle with the joy of life, Jessie Baxter Smith sought him out for an interview; for the story of his life from his own lips. The following is the story as it was carried by the press at that time:

"All genuinely great men are modest men, and Doctor Bradley is a genuinely great man. We were dependent upon his habitual kindness for the interview we had long wanted. So we started out in search of the doctor, and found him in Stone's barber shop. Sure enough, his lifelong habit of kindness won the interview for us, and in the lobby of Hotel Dalton the doctor told us many interesting things about his forefathers, and his own long, eventful life.

In Doctor Bradley's veins flows the best of English and Scots blood, and through American history his family lines runs back to Colonial days; his great grandfather, James Bradley, being a Revolutionary soldier serving with other Virginians under the command of General George Washington. After a few years of service this patriot was honorably discharged from the army because of physical disability that made it impossible to longer march and fight. In later years he recovered his robust health and died in North Carolina at the age of 103 years.

The grandfather of Doctor Bradley was an honored citizen of North Carolina, serving his State as Justice of the Peace, and as a State Legislator.

The father of the doctor was Burton Bradley, an old-fashioned Baptist preacher who married Theresa Costephens, a native of North Carolina, in 1836, and brought his family to Gordon County in Georgia in 1855, where he began his long career of preaching the Gospel, and organizing churches. He baptized many prominent people of his section, among the Reverend Wiley Dyer, an uncle of Dr. Erwin of Dalton. For his services as a Minister of the Gospel, this good man made no charges, and never received material benefit for his spiritual ministrations to his fellow beings. But while he gave himself unstintingly and without price to others, he prospered materially; rearing a large family, sending four of his children through college, and leaving at his death a highly valuable plantation. This good man also served the Cause of the Confederacy as a State Guard under command of Colonel William Dabney, of Calhoun, and was at Rome when General Forrest came to the rescue of that town against General Shields. This Baptist preacher not only gave his own service to the Cause of the South, but he gave two sons to help fight its battles. William C. Bradley went into the army under the command of Colonel Tatum Wofford, and was killed in the Second Battle of Manassas. John A. Bradley was wounded in the Battle of Atlanta captured and carried a prisoner to Rock Island Prison where he remained until 1865. Nor does this end the record. Doctor Bradley, then a little boy, contributed his share to the defense of the South by carrying half-moon pies to the soldiers who were at the back of his father's farm busy tearing up the railroad to prevent supplies being shipped to the Union soldiers.

The doctor remembers that his father's farm was completely stripped of fowls and animals, that for six months, he did not hear a rooster crow, a horse neigh, a lamb bleat, or a pig squeal. He also remembers helping to dig the dirt under the smokehouse, and seeing it dripped in order to secure the salt from it, as he remembers helping to hide the meat to keep the Yankees from capturing it.

The doctor says the hardest times he ever saw were during those terrible years immediately following the close of the Civil War. He remembers how his father's whole family went to work on the farm, and made a crop of a thousand bushels of corn with the hoe.

As an example of the honor and honesty of those brave days when men believed in God and themselves, and fought the hard realities of life with a courage and determination nothing could daunt, the doctor tells an interesting story about Judson C. Clements, who is widely remembered by the older people of this section of the State as the man who opposed Dr. Felton for Congress in that famous race when a mule colt was going to be weaned.

John Bradley and Judson C. Clements were held in Rock Island Prison at the same time, and while there Clements borrowed ten dollars from Bradley. Before it was possible for the money to be paid back, the two soldiers were separated by being released at different times. After coming home, John Bradley was teaching school near Calhoun, boarding in the home of Samuel Harlan, the great-grandfather of Dr. Trammell Starr of Dalton. James Harlan had occasion to go on a trip through the western part of the county. While on the trip he spent a night in the home of Judson C. Clements' father and mentioned that John Bradley was teaching in his neighborhood, whereupon Judson Clements told how he had been in prison with John Bradley, had borrowed ten dollars from him, and had never been able to repay it because he did know where he was located. When James Harlan came home, he delivered ten dollars to the school-teacher for Judson C. Clements, and, thus one man had discharged a debt of honor to another man.

With the blood of a long line of heroic and self-sufficient men coursing through his veins, and remembering the tragedies, strugglings, hardships, and incomparable triumphs, of days that tried the mettle of men, the boy who was to become one of Nature's own Noblemen, crowned and sceptered by her own imperial hands, could not have become anything less. He belonged to a race of Conquerors, and the labors of life could only develop the innate greatness of his being. In studying the lives of such men, we are permitted to uncover the Cause of their greatness, and name the Source from which they drew unfailing strength and courage. It was their unfaltering faith in God and in themselves.

Doctor Bradley was born in Gordon County, Georgia in 1857, and graduated from Southern Medical College (now Emory University), in 1884 with Second Honors, and here it is interesting to note that it was this young doctor who suggested the name, Folsom, for the place where he began his life work; the name being suggested to the Post Office Department in honor of President Cleveland's wife; Folsom being her maiden name.

In the year 1886, the doctor was married to Miss Ora Anna Lewis., a granddaughter of Major Lynn, and a daughter of Lieutenant H. D. Lewis who fought for the Confederacy in the siege of Vicksburg.

For years Doctor Bradley rode horseback on his long rounds of bedside visits to his patients; rode through the pelting storms and scorching heat of Summer; rode through the bitter winds and swirling snows of Winter; rode over roads that were nothing but steep and winding trails of mud and rust's rode through streams that were freezing cold; rode many times with shoes and clothes frozen on his body; rode into the hearts of multitudes of men and women and little children, and who can doubt it – rode into the Kingdom of Heaven, that Kingdom prepared for those who serve.

The doctor can tell many interesting, many soul stirring, and many amusing stories about his long years of practice as a country physician. One he told us was about a man paying him for a certain hard service rendered. The doctor had been doing this man's practice for years without collecting anything. The man coming again, told him he had some money for him this time. The doctor answered the call for help. All night, and far in to the following day, it was necessary for him to remain at the patient's bedside. When at last he was free to climb into the saddle again, the grateful man handed him three silver quarters – seventy-five cents – happy that he could pay the doctor this time for his services.

The doctor was physician to the parents of 'Pretty Boy Floyd,' and on his books is the record of his trip to their home when this ill-fated boy was born. The oldest boy in this family was named Bradley for the doctor.

When Lundy Harris, the husband of the famous Corra Harris, was fatally stricken, the doctor was called to attend him, but was away from home seeing patients. Upon returning home, he was informed of the call, and began making arrangements to answer it, then was informed that Dr. Harris was out of danger, and would not need him.

On one occasion, Doctor Bradley accompanied Corra Harris through the Mosteller Mills, showing her the old machinery, the curiously-shaped wagon beds, and the various devices used for the manufacture of cloth in the years before the War.

Once a man came to engage the doctor's service, and asked what the charge would be. The doctor told him, and the man said, 'I can get a good doctor for that.' The doctor replied 'By George, you would have a doggoned good one if you had me, but you can't get me at any price now.' When the call came, the doctor answered it.

It is a treat to see the expression on the doctor's face, and the twinkle in his dark eyes, when he tells this story:

One bitter cold night the doctor made a long trip to see a patient, and found upon reaching the patient's home, that he could not dismount. His shoes were frozen fast to the stirrups, and had to be knocked loose before the doctor could get off old Celum.

On another occasion, he was riding across the edge of a graveyard on a dark rainy night when a limb brushed his hat off. The doctor says he was not scared, but that he did not like the idea of staying long enough in that graveyard to hunt about in the dark for his hat.

The doctor says he has always been a good joiner. He has joined the Farmers' Alliance, the Odd Fellows, and the Masons.

The multitudes of men and women who have known the doctor long and well would say that all these organizations were gainers in the joining of this man whose whole life has been the embodiment of those high and sublime principles for which Oddfellowship and Masonry stand.

The doctor wears a Past Master's jewel ring presented to him when he became a Past Master of the Bartow County Masonic Convention.

The doctor declares with broad smile and twinkling eyes, that he still prefers ground travel, although he has a son and a son-in-law who are experienced pilots, owning their planes.

During his fifty-five years of practice, Dr. Bradley has seen the theory and practice of medicine revolutionized; but he has kept abreast of his beloved profession, and today with his profound knowledge, his keenness of mind, his unfailing sympathy, and unfailing kindness, he is a White Plumed Knight in the front rank of those noble men whose calling is to soothe the hurts, bind the wounds, heal the sickness, and safeguard the health of their fellow beings.

His wisdom, his kindness, his humor, his human touch, his high qualities of manhood and of citizenship, endears Doctor

214

Bradley to the people of Dalton and the surrounding counties. Well may men and women thank God for making such men."

XXVII: PHILOSOPHY OF LIFE

IN MEDIEVAL TIMES when artists painted a picture of Christ, they always painted a halo of light around His head. When they painted the picture of Apolyon, they painted a flame of fire issuing from his nostrils. It has been said, and truly, that each and every one carries with him an aura, or some kind of radiation of his soul.

Sometimes it is a halo of light, portraying the beautiful soul within and sometimes it is a flame of fire, depicting the true and hidden character of the individual. Nor does it take the artist's eye to see the halo, or the flame, that emanates from each of us.

We should strive to make it the halo of Christ shining in our lives, like a beacon of light, radiating and lighting up our way, as we pass along the road that we pass but once.

We are living between two Eternities; the Eternity of the past and the Eternity of the future. The narrow bridge that we stand on is the present. The Eternity of the past is gone forever; it is only a memory. No matter how much we may long to go back and pluck some golden moments spent with some loved one, a darling mother, a dear father, a loving companion, a precious child, it is entirely beyond our reach. Those happy hours are gone forever. This narrow bridge, the Present, is very fragile and uncertain, we have no guarantee that it will last a single hour, not even a minute, "Tomorrow's sun may never rise." We stand on this frail bridge, the Present, and peer into the Future Eternity. What does it hold in its unexplored secret chambers?

Is it tragedy, trouble, disappointment, sickness, or death? It is well that we do not know what awaits us just around the corner, or beyond the turn of the road, perhaps if we knew we would faint and fall by the wayside. But there is another Life, an Eternity that begins when this natural life ends, a spiritual life of eternal happiness, or eternal punishment.

Let us, like Abraham of old, "Look for a city with foundations whose maker and builder is God; a house of many mansions, Eternal in the Heavens; where God shall wipe away all tears, and where there shall be no more death; neither sorrow nor crying, where there shall be no night, and no need of a candle, nor light of the sun; for the Lord God is the Light, and the redeemed shall reign with Him forever and ever."

"Let not your heart be troubled, ye believe in God, believe also in me. In my Father's house are many mansions, if it were not so I would have told you. I go to prepare a place for you, and if I go and prepare a place for you, I will come again and take you unto myself, that where I am, ye may be also."

> How sweet to think, that on our eyes
> A lovelier clime shall yet arise
> That we shall wake from sorrow's dream
> Beside a pure and living stream.

CPSIA information can be obtained
at www.ICGtesting.com
Printed in the USA
LVHW110746210420
654167LV00001B/218